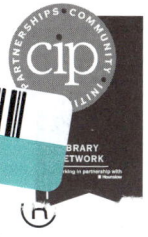

Macromedia

Flash™ 5

M I N U T E

G U I D E

que® 201 West 103rd Stre
Indianapolis, IN 46290

Joe Sullivan

Ten Minute Guide to Macromedia® Flash™ 5

Copyright © 2002 by Que® Corporation

International Standard Book Number: 0-7897-2673-4

Library of Congress Catalog Card Number: 2001093982

Printed in the United States of America

First Printing: November, 2001

04   03   02   01   4   3   2   1

Trademarks

Warning and Disclaimer

Associate Publisher
Greg Wiegand

Acquisitions Editor
Stephanie J. McComb

Development Editor
Mark Cierzniak

Managing Editor
Thomas F. Hayes

Project Editor
Karen S. Shields

Production Editor
Maribeth Echard

Indexer
Lisa Wilson

Proofreader
Melissa Lynch

Team Coordinator
Sharry Lee Gregory

Interior Designer
Gary Adair

Cover Designer
Alan Clements

Page Layout
Michelle Mitchell

TABLE OF CONTENTS

$c2/000079\ 3/02$

TELL US WHAT YOU THINK!

As the reader of this book, *you* are our most important critic and commentator. We value your opinion and want to know what we're doing right, what we could do better, what areas you'd like to see us publish in, and any other words of wisdom you're willing to pass our way.

As an associate publisher for Que, I welcome your comments. You can fax, e-mail, or write me directly to let me know what you did or didn't like about this book—as well as what we can do to make our books stronger.

Please note that I cannot help you with technical problems related to the topic of this book, and that due to the high volume of mail I receive, I might not be able to reply to every message.

When you write, please be sure to include this book's title and author as well as your name and phone or fax number. I will carefully review your comments and share them with the author and editors who worked on the book.

Fax: 317-581-4666

E-mail: feedback@quepublishing.com

Mail: Greg Wiegand
             Que
             201 West 103rd Street
             Indianapolis, IN 46290 USA

INTRODUCTION

Generations come and go very quickly in the world of Web publishing. Not all that long ago in calendar years many Web sites had a relatively static appearance. Now the Internet is bursting with sites that move, have sounds, and allow the site visitor to respond to them in a multitude of ways. Interactivity—the ability of the site visitor to direct and even control certain aspects of a Web site—is now the norm. Animation and sound are found everywhere from the most up-to-date corporate sites to family reunion pages.

These dynamic elements of Web design and construction help provide the basis for almost limitless creativity to the site builder, whether full-time professional or devoted amateur and hobbyist. They can also make the experience of Web browsing far more enjoyable, worthwhile, entertaining, and productive to the people who enter such sites.

WHAT FLASH 5 IS

Macromedia Flash is one of the most popular applications for developing dynamic sites. Just about anyone who has browsed the Internet is familiar on some level with Flash. If you have come across pages filled with energy and dynamic graphics, the chances are good that those pages were created, at least in part, using Flash.

The full potential of Flash 5 can be explored for a long time. Flash 5 provides the Web designer with a powerful set of tools and options to develop site animation and interactivity to the fullest. These can appear daunting to a Web design newcomer.

But the essential components of Flash 5 can be learned with a little effort by the newcomer, and this knowledge can be the foundation for further exploration of its many dimensions. Keep in mind the importance of experimenting with and exploring the many facets of Flash 5. As you become more confident and knowledgeable in your mastery of Flash 5, you will be able to utilize more of its many tools and components to their fullest.

Flash 5 enables a Web designer to incorporate animation and sound into the site without learning the complicated code otherwise required. Flash creations—which are called *movies* in Flash terminology—have the distinct advantage of being quick to download. They flow crisply and smoothly, and have a good presentation in any browser.

USING THIS BOOK

This book will enable the reader to become familiar with the essential components of Flash 5. Before you know it, you will have the ability to construct lively, colorful, and, above all, interesting Web pages. Even if you have never done Web design, much less dynamic Web design, you will find that Flash 5's relatively understandable interface will soon become comprehensible. The book will be helpful even as you master Flash 5 and need to look up information on some of its particular aspects.

The first two lessons of this book will introduce you to the essentials of Flash 5. You will become familiar with its environment, and meet the Flash 5 tools that enable you to create and manipulate the images that compose a Flash movie.

The core of the book is devoted to a step-by-step tour through the main components of Flash: the drawing and painting tools, the ability to move and reshape objects, the Flash stage, the layers, and text, buttons, and animation that go into making a Flash 5 movie. Finally, the concluding lessons delve into incorporating Flash into other types of Web pages.

CONVENTIONS USED IN THIS BOOK

To help you move through the lessons easily, these conventions are used:

In telling you to choose menu commands, this book uses the format *menu title, menu command*. For example, the statement "choose File, Properties" means to "open the File menu and select the Properties command."

In addition to those conventions the *10 Minute Guide to Macromedia Flash 5* uses the following icons to identify helpful information:

NEW TERM

> **Term**   New or unfamiliar terms are defined in term sidebars.

TIP

> **Tips**   Read these tips for ideas that cut corners and confusion.

CAUTION

> **Cautions**   This icon identifies areas where new users often run into trouble; these tips offer practical solutions to those problems.

Lesson 1
Meet Flash 5

In this lesson, you will be introduced to Flash 5, and learn about its purpose and capabilities.

Installing Flash 5

When you insert the Flash 5 CD-ROM into your drive, the install screen appears and begins the process of installation. Most users should accept all the defaults and install Flash according to the recommendations and instructions Macromedia suggests. To accept defaults, simply click **NEXT** throughout the installation. This is what Flash calls the Typical installation.

Along with running the Flash 5 program, the Typical installation allows you to use the Flash Libraries (which contain clip art, graphics and music files); Lessons (which contain tutorials); and Samples (which have sample movies).

Macromedia provides some important installation options. The Compact installation contains the Lessons, but not the Libraries and Samples. Custom installation allows you to select which files, lessons, samples, and library files you want to install.

After you have chosen your installation mode, Flash 5 will prompt you to install the Netscape Plug-In. This program enables Flash movies to open in the Netscape Navigator browser. Unless you are positive you don't want to view your Flash 5 movies in Netscape, click **Yes, Install the Plug-In**.

CUSTOMIZING INSTALLATION

As you learn more about Flash 5, you may want to customize your installation and change its features. To do this, reinstall Flash 5 and select different installation options.

UNDERSTAND THE BASICS OF FLASH

Flash enables the user to create images and to incorporate them, seamlessly, into movies. The viewer can often jump to a specific scene by clicking on buttons.

Flash 5's interactivity enables the site visitor not only to react to, but also to change, the scene unfolding on his or her computer screen. Figure 1.1 shows an interactive site that presents the visitor with numerous options. Hovering above a date on the left will highlight information about that date on the right of the screen.

VECTOR GRAPHICS VERSUS BITMAP IMAGES

Flash 5 creates images using vector graphics. A vector is a mathematically defined object with both quantity (size) and direction (curves, angles, and so on).

Vector graphics are easier and quicker for computers to store and download than bitmap images. Bitmap images are defined by and composed of an enormous number of tiny dots called pixels.

Vector files are smaller than bitmap files. They take up considerably less space on your computer. When you begin to learn more about how many images go into the creation of a Flash 5 movie, you will see how important this is.

Vector images have other advantages for computer graphics. They can be resized or reshaped easily without losing their form. They also have smooth edges, and maintain that quality even when enlarged. Bitmap images can get grainy and indistinct at the edges, especially when they are manipulated.

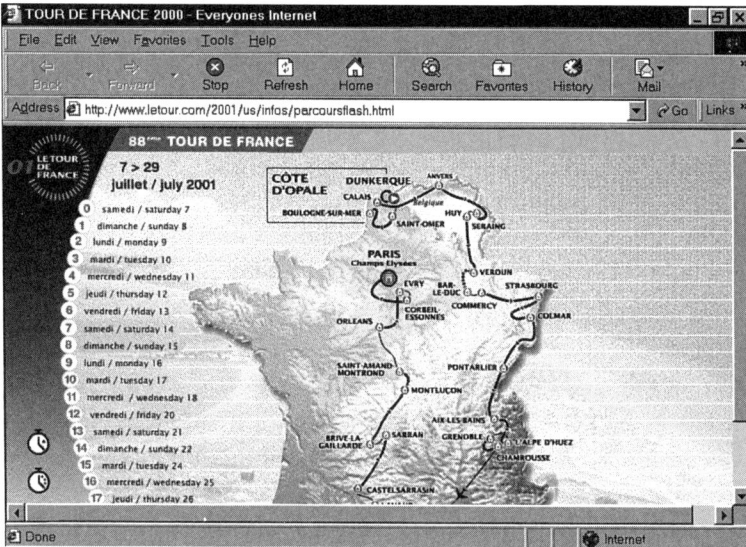

FIGURE 1.1
A complex site for the Tour de France. Interactive buttons on the left activate information on particular stages of the Tour.

VECTORS AND BITMAPS

Bitmap images are great for individual photos.

DISPLAYING WITH FLASH VIEWER

A Flash 5 movie is made of numerous frames that display sequentially. As in a conventional movie, the Flash 5 movie can display its frames quickly enough so that the entire creation unfolds smoothly. Yet, each frame, and even the components of each frame, can be broken down and manipulated by the film's producer.

Flash also has action scripting. This enables the visitor to a Flash Web site to interact with the site, often triggering motion, sound, and general change in the movie, sending a viewer to a particular part of a movie, and other changes.

NEW TERM

> **Action scripting** does not refer to any text you insert in your Flash movie. It refers to a computer programming language built into Flash. Action scripting is a big part of what makes Flash 5 special. It is what makes Flash 5 movies responsive to external prompting, such as a click by the viewer's mouse.

Flash movies are viewed through a Flash viewer. The Flash viewer enables both of Flash 5's main features—interactivity and seamless presentation of multiple frames of vector graphics—to work. A real strength of Flash movies is that the great majority of Web users can view them in their browsers.

GETTING THE FLASH VIEWER

> The Flash viewer can be downloaded free at `www.macromedia.com`.

FLASH 5 ENVIRONMENT: STAGE AND TIMELINE

The heart of the Flash 5 environment is its stage. This large white rectangle is where you create Flash movies. Open a stage by clicking **File, New**. Figure 1.2 shows a new Flash stage. You can manipulate images on the Flash 5 stage, to get exactly what you want.

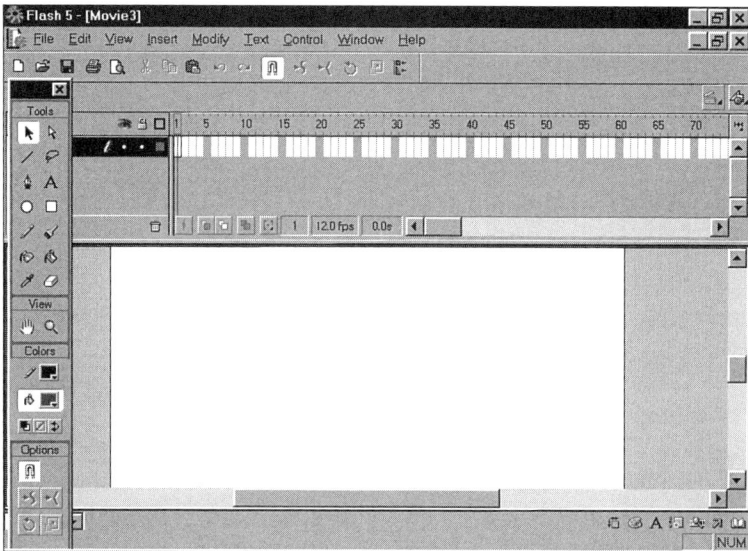

FIGURE 1.2
The Flash Stage is the white area in the middle of the screen.

Another key component of Flash is its timeline. The timeline determines when the events put on your stage will happen—their sequence, and their chronological relationship to each other. Figure 1.3 illustrates the Flash 5 timeline.

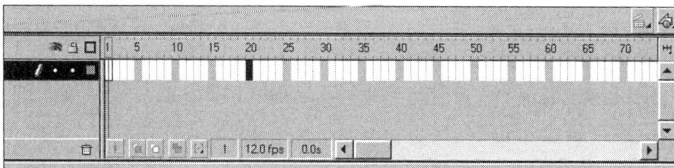

FIGURE 1.3
The numbered bar running above the stage is the Flash Timeline.

Each numbered box in the Flash 5 timeline indicates a frame that will be on the stage of your movie. A Flash 5 movie plays through the timeline frame by frame.

As you create your Flash 5 movie, you can edit any frame in the Timeline. The timeline also has a vertical readout that indicates the layers used in each frame of the timeline. Usually multiple layers go into the creation of each frame of a Flash 5 movie.

NEW TERM

> **Layers** enable the Flash user to manipulate individual objects independently of one another when creating your movie.

Learning to use the stage and the timeline is basic to learning Flash 5. It is a skill you will develop as you go through this book. It will also develop the more you use Flash 5, experiment with it, and learn a system and method that works best for you.

WHAT'S NEW IN FLASH 5

The most evident change in Flash 5 for most Flash users is its interface. It is now window (or panel) based, and thus more like other Macromedia products. The panels can be moved to suit the needs and desires of the Flash user.

You go to the panels by clicking Window and sliding down to the Panels line, as shown in Figure 1.4a. A menu with available panels drops down. Panels provide controls that enable the user to maintain close management over their creations.

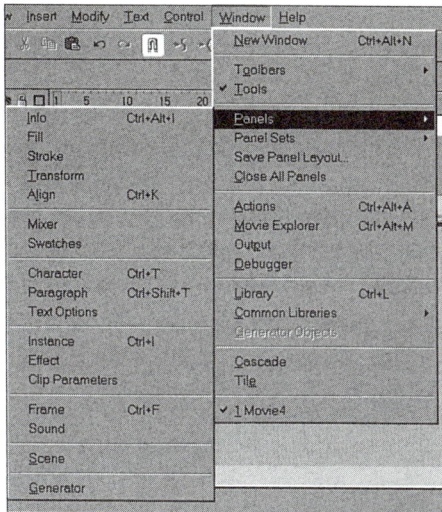

FIGURE 1.4A
Opening the Panel Menu.

You can have several panels open at once, and you can move or dock them anywhere you want on your screen. Figure 1.4b shows several panels open at once. One thing you will learn as you advance through Flash 5 is that there are often many ways to do the same task, and you will develop your own preferences.

Another major addition is a Pen tool that enables the user to make objects called Bézier curves. Bézier curves are almost perfectly smooth, and can be adjusted with nodes to achieve the precise effect the designer wants. This tool adds significantly to the creative power of the Flash 5 user. Figure 1.5 illustrates a simple Bézier curve and loop.

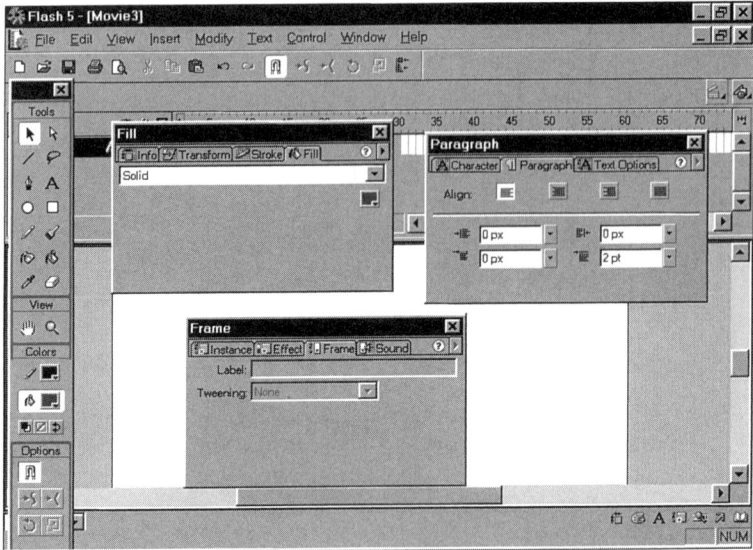

FIGURE 1.4B
Multiple panels open.

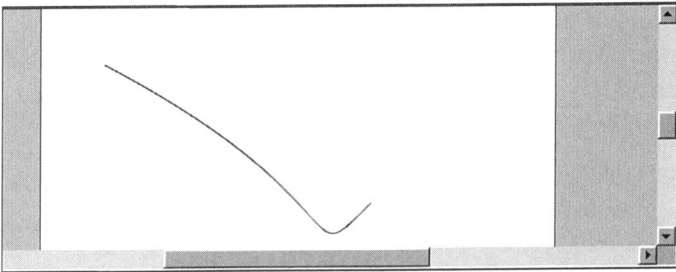

FIGURE 1.5
*A simple Bézier curve, made with the **Pen** tool.*

NEW TERM

Bézier curves are named after the French engineer who invented them. Essentially, they are curves defined by control points. In Flash 5, the user can manipulate the curve by moving any of these points.

Other changes in Flash 5 allow for easier use of its shared symbol libraries and color windows. A particularly helpful addition to Flash 5 is support for MP3 audio files. This enables the Web builder to enhance the dynamic scenes of Flash's animated movies with sound.

Flash 5 has other changes aimed more at experienced Flash users and Web designers. One of the most important is an enhanced ability to share assets in other files. These features will be more fully explored in later lessons.

LESSON 2

Exploring the Flash Environment

In this lesson, you will learn about the Flash 5 toolbox and toolbar. You will also learn about the Flash 5 control panels.

USING THE FLASH TOOLBOX

The Flash 5 toolbox is located to the left of your empty stage when you open a new Flash file. The toolbox can be moved and docked to place it wherever you want on your screen. To move the toolbox, place your cursor on a gray area in the toolbox, click and drag it to where you want to place it, and then release.

If you want to free up workspace on your stage, you can eliminate the toolbox from your screen. To do this, click the × in the upper-right corner of the toolbox. When you want the toolbox back, click **Window**, **Tools**.

Figure 2.1 shows the toolbox in isolation. It has several sections. The top section consists of the tools themselves. Select the tool you want to use by clicking it. You can see which tool is selected at any moment because a white rectangle appears around it. See Table 2.1 for the function of each tool.

FIGURE 2.1
The Flash 5 Toolbox.

TABLE 2.1 Toolbox Elements

Tool	Description
Arrow	Selects objects.
Subselect	Displays individual editing nodes within objects.
Line	Draws lines.
Lasso	Selects irregularly shaped objects of sections of your stage for editing.
Pen	Draws Bézier curves.
Text	Places typed and formatted text onto the stage.
Oval	Draws ovals and circles.
Rectangle	Draws rectangles, including squares.
Pencil	Draws freehand curved or shaped objects.

TABLE 2.1   (continued)

Tool	Description
Brush	Draws broad strokes on the stage.
Ink	Designates colors for lines.
Paint	Designates colors for filled areas.
Eyedropper	Transfers colors from one object or fill to another.
Eraser	Erases sections of a drawing.
Hand	Enables you to move a drawing around your window.
Zoom	Enables you to zoom in or out of your drawing, for a different perspective on it.

TIP

Notice that when you bring your cursor over each tool in the toolbox, a box appears with the name of the tool and a letter in parentheses. For instance, the Eraser tool has an (E). Whenever you're working in Flash 5, you can simply press one of those letters on your keyboard to select whichever tool you want to use.

Below these tools is a toolbox panel labeled Color. There are two boxes in this panel. When you hover over them with your mouse, small panels indicate that one is labeled Stroke Color and the other is labeled Fill Color. These boxes have a small arrow in their lower-right corner. Click on this arrow for a flyout of color options provided by Flash 5. Drag your pointer to a color you want and click to change either the Stroke or the Fill color.

Beneath these boxes are three other boxes. On the left is the Default Color box. Click this to restore Flash's default colors at any time. Click the middle box, No Color, to remove color from a drawing. The Swap Colors button, on the right, swaps the stroke color for the fill color.

Beneath these three boxes is an area labeled Options. The Options area varies depending on which tool is selected. For some tools, the Options area remains empty. With other tools, such as Lasso, Brush, and Eraser, different boxes appear in the area. Some of these boxes have flyouts with still further options. Figure 2.2 illustrates the Options box with the Lasso tool selected.

FIGURE 2.2
Options box for the Lasso tool.

FLASH 5 TOOLBAR

The Flash 5 toolbar looks familiar to anyone who has used Windows or Macintosh operating systems. Figure 2.3 shows the Flash 5 toolbar.

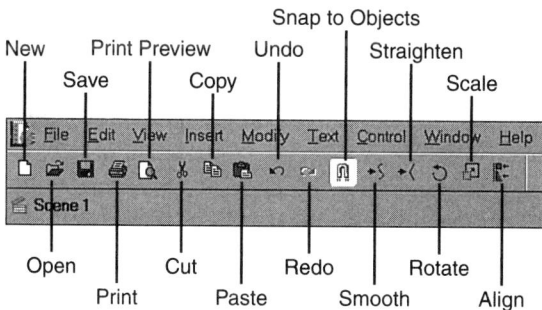

FIGURE 2.3
The Flash 5 Toolbar.

The first ten of these options are used the same way they would be on other Windows applications. The last five—**Snap to Objects**, **Straighten**, **Rotate**, **Scale**, and **Align**—have uses particular to Flash 5.

TIP

You can free up workspace by removing the toolbar when you don't need it. Go to **Windows**, **Toolbars**, and deselect the main toolbar by clicking **Main**. To replace it on your screen, do the same thing, restoring the check mark next to **Main**.

The **Snap to Objects** command enables you to align different objects on your stage precisely the way you want them to be. Different objects act as if they are "magnetized" to each other—hence the image of a magnet on the toolbar. This option can also considerably speed up the process of pasting objects onto your stage or layer.

NEW TERM

Object: Items on the Flash stage are called objects. They can be manipulated, meaning moved, deleted, copied, and otherwise transformed in various ways. They can also be made to link to URLs or to other locations in your Flash movie.

The **Smooth** and **Straighten** tools affect the editing of lines. These tools are helpful in modifying and developing your Flash 5 creations, but they also contribute to reducing file size. This is helpful in reducing the download time of your Flash 5 movie.

The **Rotate** options do exactly what their names imply. You can rotate objects around an axis with the **Rotate** tool, and get them down—or up—to size with the **Scale** tool (first, select an object).

The **Align** option enables you to place objects where you want them in relation to each other. All these Flash 5 options will be explained more fully in a subsequent lesson.

CONTROL PANELS

Control panels are the most significant single development in Flash 5, for both beginning and experienced users. Control panels enable the user to give detailed direction to the creation. To see the panels, click **Window, Panels**. A menu with a list of 17 possible Panel options is shown in Figure 2.4.

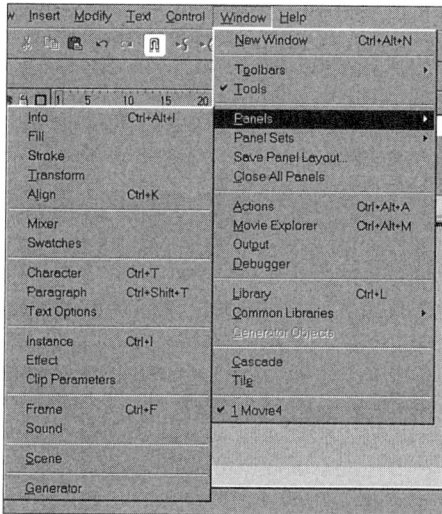

FIGURE 2.4
Opening the Panels Menu.

Control panels provide detailed information about selected objects. They also enable the user to change that information, and thus change the appearance of the object in some desired way.

From top to bottom, the panels and their basic function are as described in Table 2.2.

TABLE 2.2   Control Panel Elements

Control Panel	Description
Info	Provides the position and dimensions of selected objects.
Fill	Tells the fill types and colors of selected objects.
Stroke	Tells stroke colors and types.
Transform	Tells rotation and skewing of selected objects.
Align	Lines up objects.
Mixer	Provides info on colors, and enables users to change colors or develop new colors and color gradations.
Swatches	Enables Flash 5 users to store palettes of colors, and to create new palettes.
Character	Changes the fonts and spacing of text.
Paragraph	Another tool to modify text, by paragraph size chunks.
Text Options	Enables user to assign different qualities to selected text.
Instance	Provides ability to adjust color, and in other ways change activity (motion and sound) of Flash 5 symbols.
Effect	Enables user to further change such qualities of Flash 5 symbols as tint and brightness.
Frame	For adding labels and comments, and setting up certain types of animation.
Sound	For controlling and modifying audio in a Flash 5 movie.
Generator	Generates Web sites from movies.
Scene	For editing longer movies broken into scenes.

When you open one Flash 5 control panel, it often appears with tabs for several other panels. For instance, when you open the **Info** panel, it appears with tabs for the **Transform**, **Stroke**, and **Fill** panels. Click one of these tabs to open that panel. This way, you can work on several aspects of your movie without opening a new panel.

Flash 5 offers many ways to do similar or identical tasks. The Status Bar on the bottom of the screen enables you to quickly open frequently used panels, such as **Info**, **Mixer**, **Character**, and **Instance**. The **Zoom Box** on the left of the Status bar (see Figure 2.5) enables you to zoom in or out of the stage.

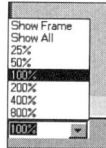

FIGURE 2.5
The Zoom Box.

LESSON 3

Drawing Images in Flash

In this lesson, you will learn how to draw lines, curves, and shapes such as ovals, circles, and rectangles. You will also learn how intersection of lines and shapes can change a Flash 5 object.

LINES

The two primary tools for drawing straight lines in Flash 5 are the **Line** tool and the **Pencil** tool.

> **NEW TERM**
>
> **Tool Strokes**: Tool strokes are lines made with the **Line** and **Pencil** tool strokes.

To use the **Pencil** tool, select it by clicking its icon in the toolbox or by pressing Y. A range of options are available when you use the **Pencil** tool. The first is Stroke Color.

To change stroke colors, click on the small arrow in the bottom-right corner of the **Stroke Color** option box to open the palette. Figure 3.1 shows the **Stroke Color** option box. Bring the cursor over the color you want, and release. When you do this, the cursor changes to a dropper icon. Note that when you release, the box in the option box changes colors. This method is used to change stroke and fill colors with other tools, not just the **Pencil** tool.

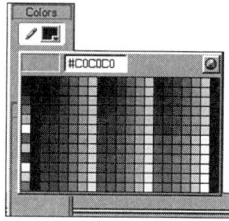

FIGURE 3.1
The Stroke Color option box.

When the **Pencil** tool is selected, a box appears in the Options panel at the bottom of the toolbox. When you hover your mouse over this box, you will see that it is labeled **Pencil Mode**. Click the arrow in the option box to display the **Pencil** options. See Figure 3.2 for an image of the options available with the **Pencil** tool selected.

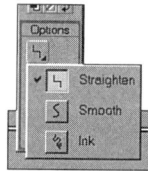

FIGURE 3.2
Pencil Tool options.

The **Straighten** option has a somewhat misleading name. It does change lines into straight lines, and is a valuable option for drawing certain shapes. It also curves jagged curves into smooth shapes. The **Smooth** option appears to work in similar fashion, but it actually removes small bumps and imperfections from lines. This can be helpful in the final stages of movie production. The **Ink** option is the closest to freeform drawing. Even here, however, Flash 5 provides antialiasing to the lines, which tends to smooth out the jagged edges of a line.

NEW TERM

Antialiasing: Antialiasing is the smoothing of transitions. It refers to the elimination of jagged edges that can mar the borders of images.

Stroke options can be further explored by opening **Window, Panels, Stroke.** The **Stroke** option box, shown in Figure 3.3, enables the user to select the stroke style, color, and height, and to see a preview of the selections. Click the arrow in the **Stroke Style** box to display the style selection. Click the arrow in **Stroke Height** to display a slider that you click and move up or down to change line thickness.

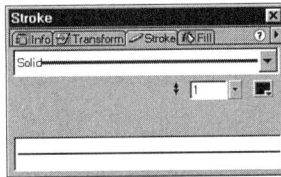

FIGURE 3.3
The Stroke option box. Stroke style is changed in the top vertical panel; stroke height in the panel beneath it.

The **Line** tool draws straight lines. After selecting the **Line** tool, click where you want your line to start. Drag and release where you want it to end. The **Stroke Panel** and the **Stroke Color** box adjust line dimensions and qualities the same way for the **Line** tool as they do the **Stroke** tool.

TIP

Holding down your Shift key as you use the line tool will constrain your lines to 45° angles.

CAUTION

Sometimes the subtlety of too elaborate stroke styles can get lost in a viewer's browser. Because of this, many Flash designers prefer to keep stroke styles relatively simple and not too detailed. Some of the more involved stroke styles work best on large, relatively simple, and straightforward graphics.

CURVES

The **Pencil** tool is best used for drawing many curves, as indicated previously. The **Pen** tool is great for drawing point-to-point curves. This can provide a wavelike effect.

To use the **Pen** tool, select it from the toolbox, and draw a vertical line on one side of your stage by clicking where you want your curve to start, dragging down, and releasing. Then, do the same on the other side of the stage. When you release, a curved line will connect your two control nodes.

NEW TERM

Nodes: Nodes in Flash are control points along or at the end of a line, curve, or shape. They can be selected and moved to alter the shape of a line or form.

Images made with the **Pen** tool often turn out a bit differently than expected. It is often best to draw an image approximating the one you want, and then edit it. To edit an image made with the **Pen** tool, use the **Select** tool. When the tool is over the end of a line, the cursor appears as a right angle. At other points of the line, it appears as an arc. In both cases, click and drag to alter the curve. Figure 3.4 shows a curve being edited by moving a control point.

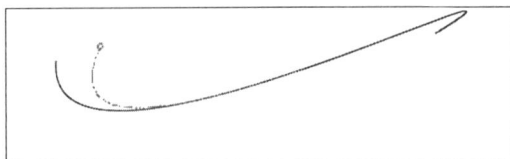

FIGURE 3.4
Editing a Bézier curve made with the Pen tool.

TIP

> To move the entire image, with the **Select** tool on, click at any point on the curve. The cursor appears as a directional box with four arrows. Click and drag to reposition your curve.

SHAPES

Ovals and rectangles can be drawn with the **Line** or **Pencil** tools. But the best tools for this purpose are the **Oval** and **Rectangle** tools. These shapes can be drawn with or without outlines. When the oval or rectangle tool is selected, the border color is determined by the stroke color, and the color of the shape's interior by the fill color. Opening the stroke panel and entering new stroke shape and height changes the qualities of the border.

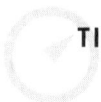

TIP

> Draw perfect circles and squares by holding down the Shift key as you draw with either the **Oval** or the **Rectangle** tool.

Figure 3.5 shows examples of an oval, circle, rectangle, and square made by the Flash 5 **Oval** and **Rectangle** tools.

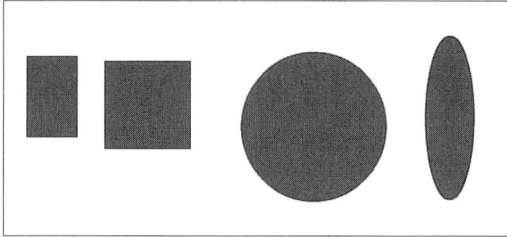

FIGURE 3.5
Rectangles, ovals, and circles can be made with Flash 5.

INTERSECTION

New objects are created when Flash shapes or lines intersect. This enables the user to cut into existing objects with another object to create a desired effect. To obtain this effect, create an image with Flash 5, select it with the **Arrow** tool, and then click and move it over another object. Then, click the second object to select it, and move it away.

In the following illustration, Figure 3.6 shows a possible use of this effect. The circle was moved over the square, which was then selected and moved away, leaving a new, changed object.

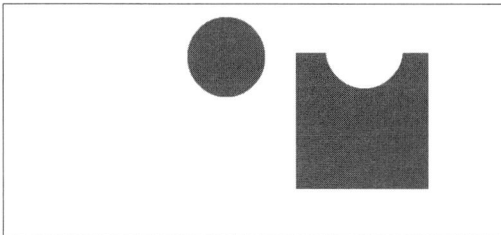

FIGURE 3.6
Flash objects can be combined to create new shapes.

Lesson 4

Painting and Erasing in Flash

In this lesson, you will learn to use the Flash 5 brush tools to create strokes, and to weave strokes in front of and behind objects. You will also learn to use the Eraser.

SELECT AND USE BRUSHES

Flash 5 provides many options when the **Brush** tool is selected. The color of a brush stroke is determined by the color selected in the **Fill Color** option box.

The bottom of the **Option Box** has options that enable the user to determine the brush size and shape. Click the arrow in either box to open that box. Figure 4.1 shows the **Brush Size** box open.

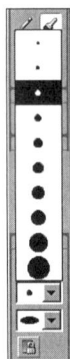

FIGURE 4.1
The Brush Size box open.

There are nine options in the Brush Shape option box. Irregular brush shapes are those that are neither square nor round, and act differently when you drag them in different directions. The effect is similar to using a wide paintbrush sideways. Figure 4.2 shows some of the effects possible using different sizes, shapes, and stroking effects with the Brush tool.

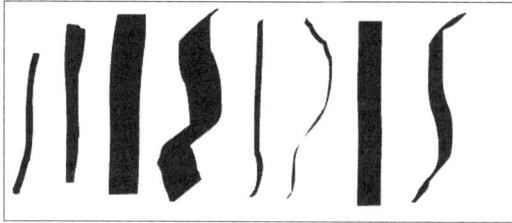

FIGURE 4.2
Examples of Brush strokes.

It is a good idea to experiment with the Brush tool to become familiar with and increasingly master its possibilities. Figure 4.3 shows a simple drawing made with the Brush tool.

TIP

> You can effectively change a brush size if for some reason the options Flash provides aren't enough for you. Changing the Zoom percentage on the Toolbar changes how broad a stroke looks on your stage. For example, a brush stroke at 100% looks twice as broad when displayed at 50%.

FIGURE 4.3
A simple drawing made with the Brush tool.

The **Brush** Tool option box also offers different effects that can be powerful components of your Flash 5 arsenal. Click the arrow in the option box to open the selections of **Paint Normal, Paint Fills, Paint Behind, Paint Selection**, and **Paint Inside**.

Paint Normal covers everything over which you move your brush. **Paint Fills** does not paint over lines (including borders), only fills. **Paint Behind** paints over the Flash 5 stage, but leaves objects unpainted. **Paint Selection** applies a new color fill to a selected object. **Paint Inside** paints over a fill upon which you begin painting, but will not paint over its lines or borders. Figure 4.4 displays the **Brush** tool options.

FIGURE 4.4
The Brush Tool Option box open.

TIP

> You can paint outside objects, on the Flash 5 stage,
> when **Paint Inside** is selected. But after you start painting
> inside an object with this selection on, you can't paint
> outside the object.

The Eraser Tool

The **Eraser** tool provides numerous modes that give the Flash 5 user a variety of options to remove objects, or parts of objects, from the stage.

The **Eraser** tool comes with a set of size and shape options similar to the **Brush** tool. With the **Eraser** tool selected, click the arrow in the **Eraser Shape** box at the bottom of the option box, and select the eraser size you want. Its image will appear in the box.

TIP

> If, instead of erasing portions of an object, you want to
> remove it entirely from the stage, it usually is best to
> delete it. You can do this by choosing the **Arrow** tool and
> clicking on the object you want to delete to select it.
> Then, just hit the Delete key.

The **Eraser** mode options, with their selections of **Normal**, **Fills**, **Lines**, **Selected Fills**, and **Inside**, are similar to the **Brush** tool's mode options. In both cases, the function of the tool changes somewhat depending on the option selected.

Normal mode erases everything over which you pass the eraser. **Fills** and **Lines** modes erase only fills and lines, respectively. To use **Selected Fills** mode, first select an object with the **Arrow** tool. Then, use the **Eraser** tool with this mode selected to erase only within that selected fill. Even if you seem to be erasing more as you pass over the object, the area outside the selected fill will reappear when you release the mouse. **Erase Inside** removes fills from the object on which you begin using the eraser.

> **TIP**
>
> To remove everything from the stage, double click the **Eraser** tool. If you do this (or take any other action you immediately want to reverse) inadvertently, click the **Undo** button on the Flash 5 toolbar.

Figure 4.5 shows the option box of the **Eraser** tool, with its various modes.

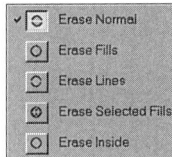

FIGURE 4.5
The Eraser Tool option box.

> **CAUTION**
>
> It isn't hard to erase more than you intend to. If this happens, you can reverse the damage by selecting **Edit, Undo**. If you want to go back to the original look before you selected Undo, choose **Edit, Redo** from the toolbar.

Another important aspect of the **Eraser** tool is its **Faucet** option. Activate this option by clicking the faucet icon, with the **Eraser** tool selected.

The cursor changes into a faucet, with a tiny drop coming out of it. Place the drop over the area you want to erase and click to remove it. Figure 4.6 illustrates a border about to be removed from an oval.

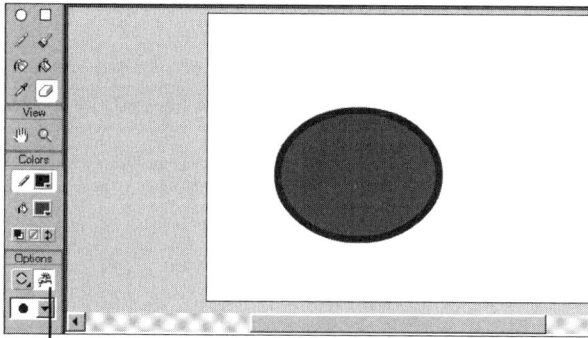

Erasing with the Faucet tool

FIGURE 4.6

Erasing with the Faucet tool. When the mouse is clicked, the border will be removed, and the fill will remain.

LESSON 5
Filling Objects with Color

In this lesson, you will learn to select, change, and blend colors. You will also learn to use transparency, and to fill with the Paint Bucket.

SELECT AND CHANGE COLORS

As you saw in an earlier lesson, Flash 5 comes with well-equipped palettes. The standard palette has 256 browser-safe colors.

However, you may want to create your own colors, or to use a smaller palette. A smaller palette can be helpful in situations in which you want to use a certain color scheme for your project, or part of your project.

To change the color palette, select **Window**, **Panels**, **Mixer** to open the **Mixer** panel. First, select the color you want by clicking on the desired area in the color bar at the bottom of the box. Then, open the flyout menu by clicking the arrow near the upper-right corner of the box. Figure 5.1 shows the **Mixer** panel with the flyout box open.

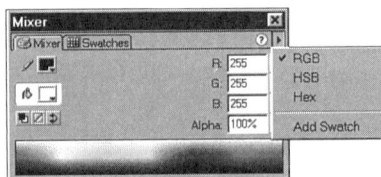

FIGURE 5.1
The Mixer panel with the flyout box open.

Then, click **Add Swatch** from the flyout. You can also add a color by changing the values in the RGB box to get the color you want. Then, open the flyout and click **Add Swatch**.

To customize your palette, open the **Swatches** panel by selecting **Window, Panels, Swatches**. Open the menu options by clicking the upper-right arrow. Figure 5.2 shows the **Swatches** menu options.

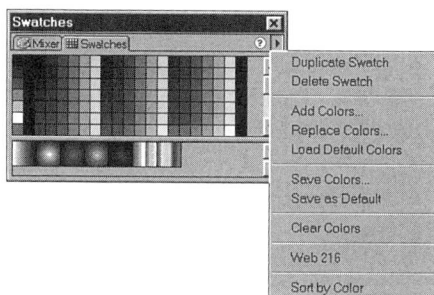

FIGURE 5.2
The Swatch panel options.

Clicking **Clear Colors** removes all colors except a black-to-white gradient from your swatch. (You can restore them at any time by clicking **Web 216**.) With all colors removed, add or create a color in the **Mixer** panel by one of the methods outlined previously. Remember to finish the task by clicking **Add Swatch**. Your new color now appears in the **Swatches** panel.

To save a custom palette, choose **Save Colors** from the **Swatches** options flyout. The **Export Color Swatch** dialog box appears. In the

Save As Type box, select **Flash Color Set (*.clr)**. Type in a name for your palette, select your folder, and click **Save**. Figure 5.3 shows the **Export Color Swatch** dialog box.

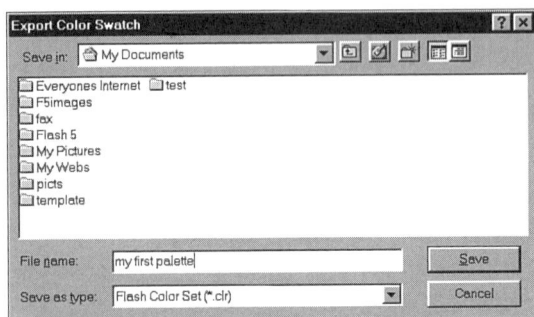

FIGURE 5.3
The Export Color Swatch dialog box.

You can use a custom palette as your default palette by selecting **Save As Default** from the Swatch box flyout.

BLEND COLORS

Blended colors, or colors that merge into each other, are called gradients. Linear gradients change in color from one side of an object to the other, whereas radial gradients start in the center and move outward. Figure 5.4 shows examples of ovals with each type of gradient.

The bottom line of the **Fill Color** palette comes with several predetermined gradients. Click on them to use them with the **Fill** option.

Define a custom gradient by selecting **Window**, **Panels**, **Fill**. Click the downward-pointing arrow to open the Options flyout, and select either radial or linear gradient.

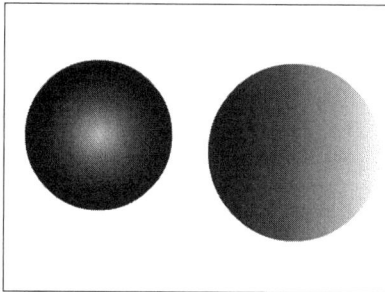

FIGURE 5.4
Gradients: A radial gradient is on the left; a linear gradient on the right.

The horizontal bar with bucket icons hanging on it edits the gradient range. Click and drag the icons in either direction on the bar to adjust the gradient to one you desire, or click and drag downward to remove a color from the gradient. Add icons by clicking just below the bar. Figure 5.5 shows the **Fill** panel.

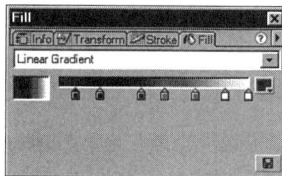

FIGURE 5.5
The Fill panel, with bucket icons determining gradient.

NEW TERM

Gradients: Gradients can add substantially to file size, thus making your movie take longer to download in many visitors' browsers. Keep this in mind and try to keep your use of gradients in check as you develop your movies.

To change a color in a pointer, click the pointer, click the arrow in the **Gradient Pointer** box to the right of the gradient bar, and select the color. Up to eight colors can be assigned to a gradient. Save a gradient by clicking the **Save** icon in the lower right of the **Fill Panel**.

TIP

> The **Paint** tool can't change the color of the entire stage. If you want to change the Stage color, select **Modify, Movie** from the toolbar to open the **Movie Properties** dialog box. Click on the arrow in the **Background Color** square to open a palette, and select the new color. Click **OK**, but be aware that this will change the background for your entire movie, not just the frame or scene in which you are working.

TRANSPARENCY

A helpful Flash quality is the **Alpha** slider, which defines the solidity and transparency of the color of filled objects. The **Alpha** slider is in the **Mixer Panel**, beneath the RGB values. An **Alpha** setting of 100% means the fill will be completely solid; the lower the setting, the greater the transparency.

If an image is defined with a greater degree of transparency, objects moved behind the shape will show through.

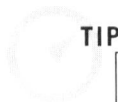

TIP

> Transparency can be effective, but try not to overdo it. It can slow down the movie playback.

THE PAINT BUCKET, INK BOTTLE, AND DROPPER TOOLS

The **Paint Bucket** allows you to change the color of an existing shape. Select the **Paint Bucket**, select the color (or gradient) you want, and click on the shape you want to recolor.

Options in the **Paint Bucket** flyout allow you to choose how to fill in the gaps in the shape. **Don't Close Gaps** will only fill enclosed areas. **Close Large Gaps** will fill shapes that aren't completely enclosed. The other selections are between these two.

The **Ink Bottle** works similarly, but to change line color. Change a line color by selecting a color from the **Stroke Color** area of the tool-box. Then, select the **Ink Bottle** tool, drag to the line you want to change, and click.

The **Dropper** takes color from one fill and places it in another fill. Select the **Dropper** tool, place it over the shape with the color you want to fill it with, and click. The cursor then changes to a paint bucket, with a lock nearby. The lock indicates that a color is set in the dropper. Click on the shape whose color you want to change. Figure 5.6 shows a filled **Dropper** tool about to transfer its color to another object.

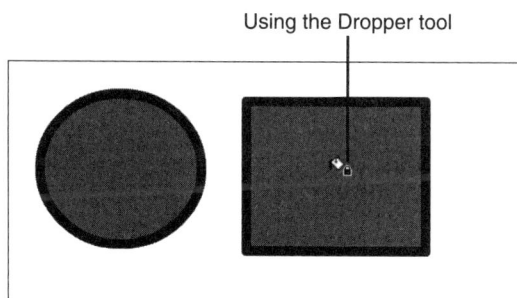

Using the Dropper tool

FIGURE 5.6
The Dropper tool is about to transfer fill color from the oval into the fill of the rectangle.

Lesson 6

Selecting and Manipulating Objects

In this lesson, you will learn to select objects with different Flash 5 tools, and begin to reshape and manipulate them.

Using the Arrow Tool

Developing a Flash movie requires considerable moving, editing, and rearranging of its components. The **Arrow** tool is one of the primary tools used for this purpose.

You've learned that clicking the **Arrow** tool and then clicking on an object selects that object. The color of the selected object dims slightly but visibly, and a directional cursor appears inside it. Hold the mouse button and drag the object to where you want it, and then release. To deselect an object, click outside its area.

The **Arrow** tool cursor takes other forms. Notice that as you drag the cursor toward an object, the shape nearby it changes from a box to an arc when the arrow tip is on the edge of the object's line. When the arrow tip is on a corner of an object, the nearby icon changes to a right angle.

When the arc is visible, click and drag on the line to change its shape. When the right angle is visible, click and drag to change direction and length of a line. Figure 6.1 shows a shape that has not been altered, and an identical shape with alterations made with the **Arrow** tool.

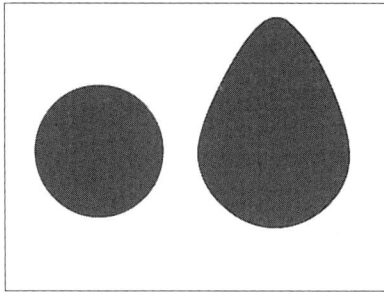

FIGURE 6.1

The figure on the right was identical to the figure on the left until it was altered with the Arrow tool.

TIP

> Even a simple image created with Flash can have many objects within it. For instance, an oval with a small border is at least two objects. If you click on the fill, the border will not be selected and will not move with the fill when you drag the cursor. To select adjacent objects, such as a fill and border, double-click. Figure 6.2 shows a shape and its border moved without double-clicking, and another being moved with double-clicking. Also, note that a border may be made up of different segments, each of them a different object.

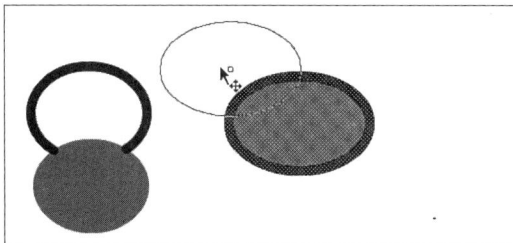

FIGURE 6.2

Two images being moved. The image on the left was moved without double-clicking; the image on the right was double-clicked and will be repositioned on the outline shape.

The Arrow tool also selects by surrounding an object or objects with a line. To select objects this way, click the Arrow tool, and then bring the point of the cursor arrow to where you want your selection to begin. Click and drag, and a box shape begins to follow your cursor. Release where you want the selection to end.

Note that this method enables you to select a portion of an object (or objects). Figure 6.3 shows a shape that has been partially selected, and then the selected part of it moved.

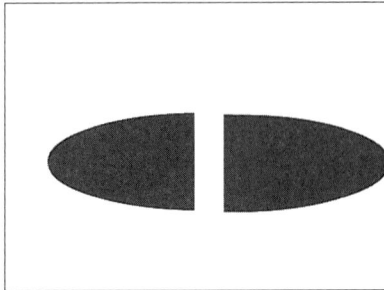

FIGURE 6.3
An oval and border that were partially selected and moved with the Arrow tool.

SELECT MULTIPLE OBJECTS

Select multiple objects by holding down the Shift key while you point and click at objects on your stage. You can then apply any changes uniformly to all these objects.

You can also select or deselect all the objects on your stage. From the Toolbar, choose **Edit**, **Select All**, or **Edit**, **Deselect All**. Then, you can apply the changes you want to the objects. Figure 6.4 shows the **Deselect All** menu option.

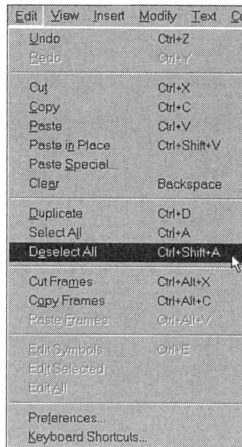

FIGURE 6.4
Deselect All on the Edit Menu.

USING THE LASSO TOOL

The **Lasso** tool is useful for selecting irregularly shaped objects. Click the **Lasso** tool and draw a freehand outline around the Stage objects you want to include in your selection. Bring the cursor back to the starting point, and release the mouse. Figure 6.5 shows several objects and portions of objects selected with the **Lasso** tool.

FIGURE 6.5
Using the Lasso tool to select all or parts of several objects on the Flash stage.

The **Lasso** tool contains a **Polygon** option. Activate this option by clicking the bottom-left box of the option box when the **Lasso** tool is activated. The **Polygon** option works by clicking nodal points connected by straight lines around your selected area.

With the **Polygon** option selected, click where you want to set your starting point. Drag the mouse, with the line trailing behind it, to the next nodal point, and click again. Continue with this until you have engirded the area you want to select, and double-click to enclose the now selected area. Figure 6.6 shows an object with several parts about to be surrounded with the **Polygon** option of the **Lasso** tool.

TIP

> You can select more intricate groupings of objects with the **Lasso** tool. First, select one group with the **Lasso** tool as previously indicated. Then, hold down the Shift key and select another group with either the **Lasso** or the **Select** tool.

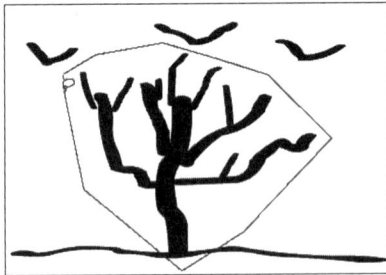

FIGURE 6.6
Using the Polygon option to select an irregularly shaped image with several parts.

CAUTION

It's not hard to get confused about which objects are
selected and which are not. Selecting the fill of an
object will not select its outline. And, when using the
Lasso tool, make sure the marquee encircles the entire
area you want to select. Unselected areas, meaning
those areas outside the marquee, become new objects,
and won't have the changes you are making applied to
them.

TIP

The other options in the **Lasso** option box are best used
with bitmapped images, not with the smooth vectors
made with Flash 5 tools. Bitmap images will be discussed in a later lesson.

LESSON 7

Grouping and Manipulating Objects

In this lesson, you will learn to group objects, and to manipulate or edit selected objects.

GROUPING OBJECTS

Even a simple Flash drawing, such as a square with a small border, is made up of more than one object. More complex figures can have many objects within them.

Flash 5 enables users to combine, or group, objects. For the purpose of editing them and moving them, they become one object. Group a set of objects by selecting them with either the **Arrow** or **Lasso** tool. Then choose **Modify, Group** from the toolbar. To ungroup selected objects, choose **Modify, Ungroup**. Figure 7.1 shows the selection to make to group objects.

If you click and drag on any object within a selected group, the entire group will move. The shapes in the grouped selection will retain the same position in relation to each other, but their position on the Stage will be moved.

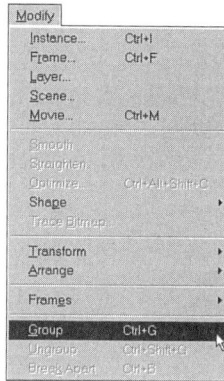

FIGURE 7.1

Select Modify, Group to group a number of objects on the stage.

TIP

> You can also edit a single object *within* a group. To edit a single grouped object, choose **Edit**, **Edit Selected** from the toolbar. Figure 7.2 shows the **Edit Selected** option. Next, click outside the selected area. Now click the **Arrow** tool and select the single object you want to edit within the group. Manipulate it as you want. Then, choose **Edit**, **Edit All** from the toolbar to reestablish the group relationship.

FIGURE 7.2

Choose Edit Selected to manipulate single objects within a group.

When grouped objects are exactly as you want them, you can lock them into place. This is helpful if you are continuing to edit a Flash 5 layer, but want to ensure that certain images remain untouched. To lock grouped objects, choose **Modify**, **Arrange**, **Lock**, from the toolbar. Figure 7.3 shows the **Modify**, **Arrange**, **Lock** selection.

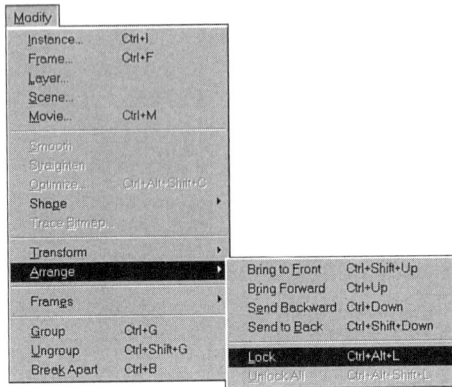

FIGURE 7.3
Locking grouped objects enables you to edit other elements of a Layer without disturbing the locked objects.

Grouped objects don't cut into each other the way ungrouped Flash 5 objects do. This enables you to stack them one on top of another in a single Flash 5 layer.

To place a grouped image (or images) on top of another grouped image, first select the grouped object(s) with the **Arrow** tool. Then, choose **Modify, Arrange** from the toolbar. Several options are presented.

- **Bring to Front** moves the group selected in front of all other grouped objects on the stage.

- **Bring Forward** moves the selected group up one level in the stacking order of groups.

- **Send Backward** moves the selected group down one level in the stacking order.

- **Send to Back** moves the selected group object behind all the other groups on the stage. Figure 7.4 shows an example of grouped images moved in front of and behind one another.

FIGURE 7.4
There are three grouped objects in this image: the rectangle and border, the oval and border, and the hockey player. They were arranged so that the oval is on top of the border, and the hockey player on top of the oval.

EDITING OBJECTS

The **Subselect** tool is a powerful new addition to Flash 5. It enables you to provide fine-tuned editing of images by moving their nodal points.

Select an image you want to edit, and then choose the **Subselect** tool from the Toolbox (or press the letter **A** on your keyboard). Notice that nodal points appear around the image, as shown in Figure 7.5.

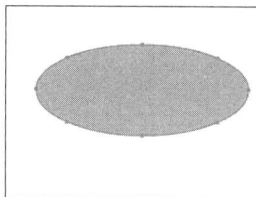

FIGURE 7.5
Nodal points that enable fine-tuned editing appear when you use the Subselect tool on a selected object.

Moving individual cursor nodes changes the image. Click on a node at a point you want to change the image. The cursor changes to a small square. Drag to change the image to a new one, and release when you have what you want. You can move as many nodes as you want. Figure 7.6 shows an image manipulated with the **Subselect** tool.

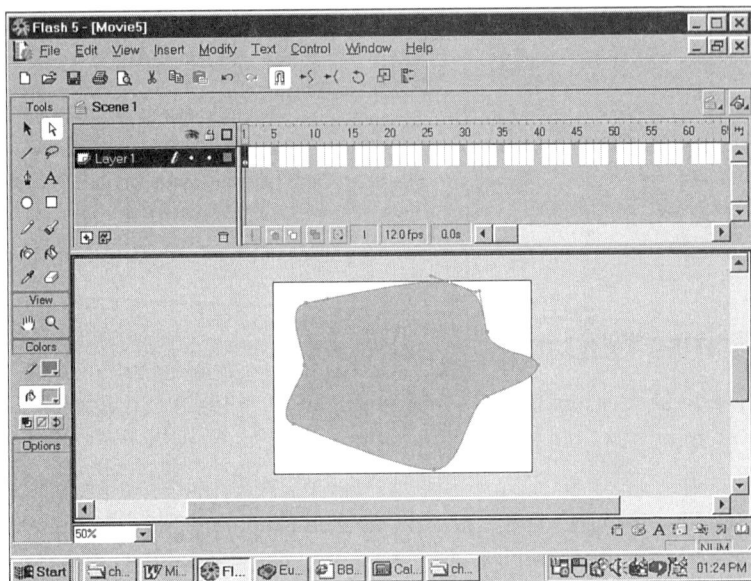

FIGURE 7.6
The oval in the previous figure has been transformed with the Subselect Tool.

TIP

> If you click on an arrow of the selected image between the nodal points, you can move the entire image, as you would with the **Arrow** tool.

The **Subselect** tool is also useful in fine-tuning curves made with the **Pen** tool. The nodal points along the Bézier curve made with the **Pen** tool can be selected and moved in the desired direction.

Editing a Bézier curve can be valuable in the final stages of your design, but be aware that, as when drawing with the **Pen** tool, editing it sometimes ends up with an image somewhat different from what you may expect. It is good to experiment with this effect to become familiar with it. Figure 7.7 shows a Bézier curve being edited with the **Subselect** tool.

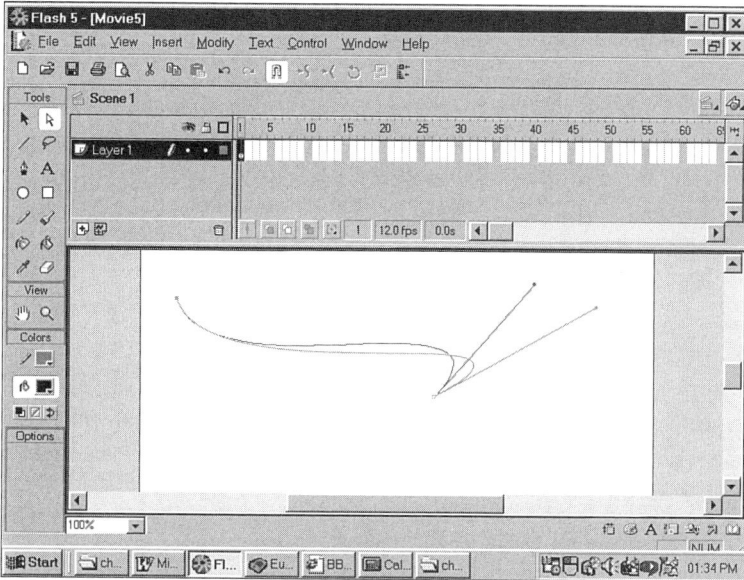

FIGURE 7.7
Editing a Bézier curve can sometimes lead to unexpected results.

TIP

Zooming in for a very close-up view can help in editing Bézier curves. The **View** drop-down menu in the status bar enables you to zoom up to 400%. You can go even higher, up to 2,000%, by entering your own numbers.

LESSON 8
The Flash Stage

In this lesson, you will learn about Stage elements, and how to use guides such as grids and rulers to position your objects on the stage. You will be introduced to Stage design.

UNDERSTANDING THE FLASH STAGE

The Flash 5 stage can be customized to best suit your purposes. This is particularly helpful as your movies and sets of shapes become more complex. Learning how to customize your stage will help you align objects with one another, position them precisely where you want them on the stage, fine-tune object size, and develop and change the background.

Stage elements for assisting the design and location of objects are Rulers, Grid lines, Customizable Guidelines, and the Snap features.

RULERS, GUIDES, AND SNAPS

The rulers are helpful in determining object size. Click **View**, **Rulers** from the toolbar. A horizontal ruler appears above the stage, a vertical ruler on stage left.

You can pull ruler lines onto the stage to help align objects. Click on the edge of the ruler and drag to where you want to align your objects, and then release it. A guideline will appear across your screen. Figure 8.1 shows an image being positioned at 100 on the horizontal ruler and 50 on the vertical.

FIGURE 8.1
Drag one or both rulers onto the stage to help position objects.

TIP

Ruler units of measurement are set to pixels. Choosing Modify, Movie from the toolbar, and selecting inches, points, centimeters, or millimeters from the Ruler Unit options can change the units.

The Ruler can be used with a snap effect to get objects exactly on the lines you want. First, have the rulers displayed and drag one or both to the places you want to serve as guidelines. Select **View**, **Guides**, and make sure both **Guides** and **Snap to Guides** are checked.

With the Snap effect activated, when you select an object and move it slowly toward the ruler line, the line will act as a magnet that snaps the object to it.

To control the intensity of the snap, go to **View**, **Guides**, **Edit Guides**. The **Edit Guides** box that appears is shown in Figure 8.2 The Snap Accuracy drop-down box displays three levels of snap intensity, Can Be Distant being the strongest. Must Be Close has the least pull.

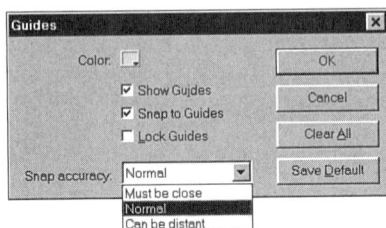

FIGURE 8.2
The Edit Guides Box adjusts snap intensity.

Grids are another way to measure and locate objects. Choose **View**, **Grid**, **Show Grid**. A grid box then covers the entire stage. The grid snap works basically the same way as the ruler snap. One big difference is that there are many more places to which to snap, or set, your objects.

To use the grid for alignment, make sure the **Snap to Grid** selection is checked. Choose **View**, **Grid**, **Snap to Grid**. When you select an object, and the snap is on, a circle appears within the object near the cursor. This circle indicates where the object will snap to the grid. Figure 8.3 shows an object about to snap to the grid.

TIP

> Animation is essentially the process of changing the location of objects from one frame to another. Using grids and rulers helps you position the objects exactly as you want them and facilitates smooth animation.

You can also change the color of the ruler or grid guidelines. This can be helpful if you have a background color other than the white stage, and you are having difficulty viewing the lines.

To change the color, choose **View**, **Grid**, **Edit Grid**, or **View**, **Guides**, **Edit Guides**. In both cases, a panel appears with a palette near the top from which you can select another color through the same method you use with any Flash palette.

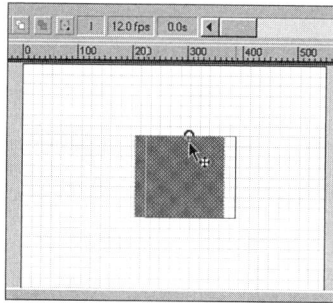

FIGURE 8.3
Snapping an object to a grid. The small circle indicates where the object will snap.

> **TIP**
>
> Keep in mind that neither the ruler nor the grid guide-
> lines will appear in your movie. They are there to help
> you design your stage.

The **Edit Guides** dialog box has a check box labeled **Lock Guides**.
This enables you to lock in the location of defined guidelines. To
move locked guides later, just uncheck the dialog box.

STAGE SIZE AND BACKGROUND COLOR

Stage size affects how a movie will be displayed in a viewer's
browser, and the overall size of a movie. A larger stage provides more
space for creative design, but also requires a larger file for downloading, and possibly takes up more of the viewer's time.

When your Flash 5 movies are seen in a Web browser, only those elements on the stage will display. The objects in gray will not be seen.
Figure 8.4 shows two images, one of which will be visible in the
movies and one of which won't.

You can determine the size of your Stage, and thus control the way
a Flash 5 movie is displayed in a Web browser or using the Flash

viewer. Generally, it is good to have the Stage large enough to encompass everything you draw, but not larger than the viewer's screen can display.

FIGURE 8.4
The drawing on the Stage will appear in the Flash movie; the object in the gray area will not.

To change movie size so that it includes everything on the stage, select **Modify**, **Movie**, and then click **Contents** in the dialog box. Figure 8.5 shows the **Movie Properties** dialog box. This procedure will reduce the size of the stage to only enough space to contain its contents.

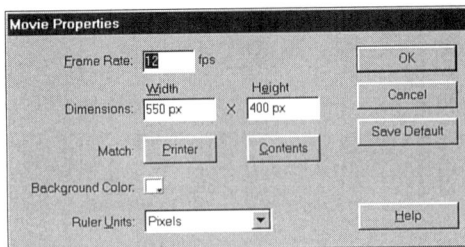

FIGURE 8.5
You can change movie size in the Movie Properties dialog box.

CAUTION

A stage that's too small won't display all the objects you may want. But too large a stage—one larger than the viewer's browser window or monitor screens—means that viewers won't see the whole movie. It won't fit in their screen. Learning to size your stage is an important part of developing your Flash 5 skills.

MOVIE BACKGROUND

Specific backgrounds can be developed for objects or scenes within movies. But you can change the background color for the entire movie you are working on by choosing **Modify**, **Movie**, to get the **Movie Properties** dialog box. Then, click the arrow in the **Color** box to get to the background palette. If you change the background color, that means the new color you have selected will be the default background for all the frames and layers in your movie. In other words, it changes for the entire movie.

LESSON 9

Learning to Use Layers

In this lesson, you will learn to use layers to position objects in front of and behind one another. You will learn how to add new layers, how to lock layers, how to use layers as guides, and how to create layers that display part of other layers.

INSERTING AND SELECTING LAYERS

Layers are arranged one on top of another within each frame of a Flash 5 movie. Layers allow you to manipulate and manage various elements of a movie without disturbing anything you don't want to. Layers can be an extremely valuable and part of developing a movie.

TIP

It's a good idea to create as many layers as you need. Each element of a movie that you want to keep apart from other elements of the movie for purposes of editing should have its own layer.

In Figure 9.1, each component of the scene is on a separate layer. The skaters are on one layer, the ice on another, and the crescent moon a third.

To open a new layer, choose **Insert**, **Layer** from the toolbar. You can also click the plus sign at the lower-left corner of the layer box. Figure 9.2 shows the insert layer icon in the layer box.

FIGURE 9.1
Each component—the dancers, the ice, and the moon—of this simple scene has its own layer.

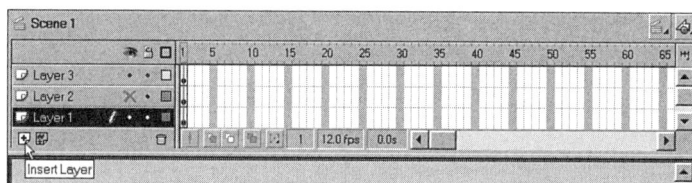

FIGURE 9.2
Add a layer by clicking on the plus sign in the layer box.

TIP

> You can change the name of a layer by double-clicking in the layer name box and typing in a new one. A good naming system helps keep track of objects in multilay-ered frames.

To select a layer, click on its name in the layer box. This also selects everything on the stage of that layer. Figure 9.3 shows the "dancers" layer selected. The dancers have been repositioned to look as if they were leaping off the ice.

Lock
Eye | Rectangle

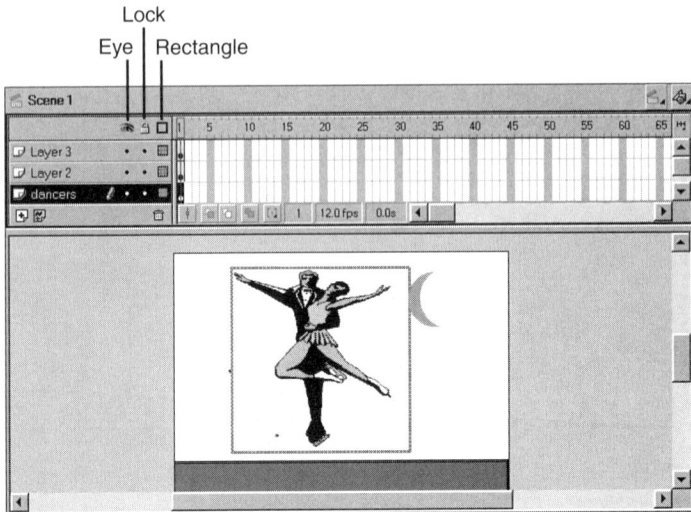

FIGURE 9.3

The layer "dancers" has been selected, as indicated by the highlighted bar in the layer box. The object with the dancers has also been selected and moved, as indicated by the box around the object.

DISPLAYING LAYERS

There are three icons across the top of the layer box: an eye, a lock, and a rectangle. These features of the layer box determine how layers are displayed, and if they can be edited. Each of these features can be clicked at the top of the layer box, and will then affect all layers; or they can be clicked layer by layer, and turned on and off individually.

- The eye icon is for the **Show/Hide** effect. It allows you to display or hide a particular layer. This is helpful in editing single layers.

- The lock is for the **Lock/Unlock** effect. If the lock is on, it prevents you from inadvertently editing a layer you don't want to touch.

- The rectangle is for the **Show As Outline** effect, which displays selected layer(s) as outlines.

- The trash can icon at the bottom of the box is for deleting layers. To delete a layer, select it, and then click the trash can.

CAUTION

Use this effect carefully. Only clicking **Undo** shortly after deletion can restore a deleted layer. Locking a layer does not prevent deletion.

REPOSITIONING LAYERS

To move layers in front of or behind one another, change their order in the layer list. Click and drag a layer to the desired position.

To move an object from one layer to another, first select the object with the **Arrow** or **Lasso** tool. Choose **Edit**, **Copy** or **Edit**, **Cut**. The object is now in the Clipboard. Select the layer in which you want to place your object, and choose **Edit**, **Paste**.

GUIDE LAYERS AND MASK LAYERS

Guide layers help you position objects on the stage. They do not appear in the movie. Any layer can be made into a guide layer, and guide layers can be changed back into ordinary layers.

To create a guide layer, select the layer, and then select **Modify**, **Layer** from the menu. The **Layer Properties** dialog box appears, as shown in Figure 9.4. Click in the **Guide** option box. A layer selected as a guide layer will have a right angle in its box.

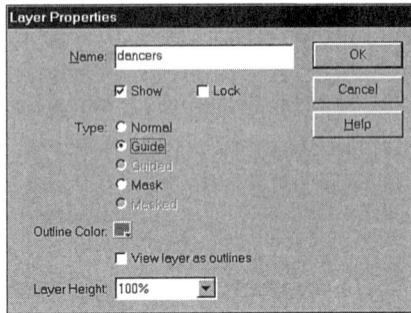

FIGURE 9.4
Changing a layer to a Guide Layer.

TIP

After you have created a guide layer, it is a good idea to lock it. This prevents accidentally moving objects you intend to serve as guides for objects on other layers. You can always unlock it, just as you can always change the guide layer to a normal layer.

Mask Layers reveal objects beneath them, much like eye holes in a mask reveal the eyes. Mask layers go above a layer (or layers) being masked. Interesting results can be achieved with this effect.

To create a Mask layer, first select **Insert**, **Layer** from the menu. Make sure the new layer that is to be your mask is on top of the layer list. Rename the layer to indicate it is your mask.

Next, draw a filled shape on the Mask layer. This shape is to act as the hole in the mask. Figure 9.5 shows an oval on a Mask layer above the drawing of the tree and birds you saw earlier.

When the shape is complete, open the **Layer Properties** dialog box for the new Mask layer, and click the button to indicate this will be a Mask layer. View the effect by locking the Mask layer. Figure 9.6 shows the effect of the Mask on the tree and birds.

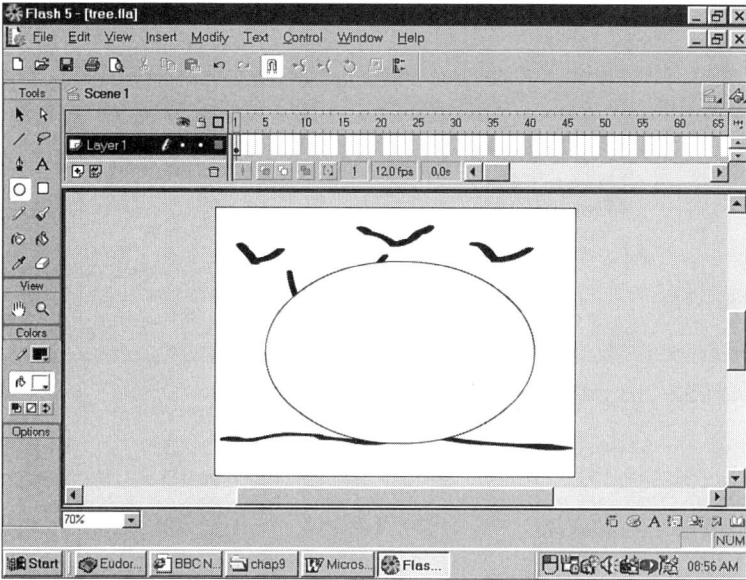

FIGURE 9.5
The oval in the top-level mask layer will act as the hole in the mask, revealing what is beneath the mask.

FIGURE 9.6
The area covered by the shape on the Mask layer is revealed when the Mask layer is locked.

TIP

Link multiple layers by opening the **Layer Properties** dialog box and selecting the Masked option. Then, arrange the layers to achieve the effect you desire. Unlink layers by the same method of clicking in the **Layer Properties** box.

Lesson 10

Adding Text to a Movie

In this lesson, you will learn to add text to a Flash movie, to change text attributes, and to shape text.

PLACING TEXT IN A MOVIE

To place text in a movie, select the **Text** tool, either by clicking on the toolbox or typing the letter **T**. With the **Text** tool selected, a letter **A** appears near the cursor as you drag it across the stage.

Click where you want your text to start, drag, and release the mouse where you want the text to end. A box will appear. This box will expand to contain the text you insert into it. Figure 10.1 shows a box created by the **Text** tool.

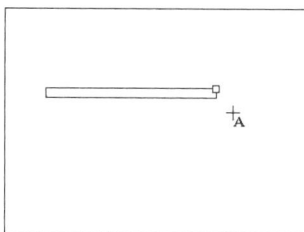

FIGURE 10.1
An empty box ready for typing text into it. The box will expand to accommodate the text.

SELECTING AND CHANGING TEXT ATTRIBUTES

Text attributes can be selected from the **Character** panel. Select
Window, Panels, Character. You can select from a wide variety of
fonts, and choose text color from a palette. Define the size of your text
in this panel by moving the slider to increase or decrease font size.
You can also select bold or italic text by clicking on the B and I buttons in the panel. Figure 10.2 shows some formatted text, with the
Characters panel open.

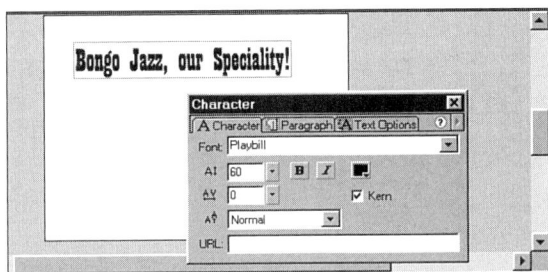

FIGURE 10.2
Some formatted text, and the Character panel open. Text attributes can be deter-
mined and changed in the Character panel.

To create paragraphs with longer blocks of text, select the **Text** tool
and desired properties as previously outlined. Click where you want
the text to begin and drag to the desired width. Text will wrap down
when it reaches the end of the box, and expand to the height needed to
accommodate your paragraph.

To resize the width of the text block, click inside the block with the
Text tool activated. The resize handle will appear, and it can be
dragged to the desired location.

To select all text in a text block for editing, use the **Text** tool and click
inside the text block. This places the cursor inside the text block.
Then, choose **Edit, Select All** from the toolbar. To select specific characters or words within a text block, place the cursor inside the block,

and then click and drag to select the characters or words you want to edit. Figure 10.3 shows a word inside a text block being edited.

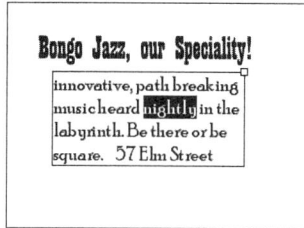

Bongo Jazz, our Speciality!

innovative, path breaking music heard nightly in the labyrinth. Be there or be square. 57 Elm Street

FIGURE 10.3
The highlighted word in the text block is being edited.

Scaling, rotating, and skewing effects can be applied to text (and other objects as well).

- Scaling alters the shape of the text—if the height increases, the text will become thinner. If the height is reduced, the text will become bulkier.

- Rotated text is like any other rotated Flash 5 object. The angle of the selected object changes to one you desire.

- Skewing pulls and slants an object to give it a different perspective. Figure 10.4 shows examples of all three effects.

To select these effects, first select the text object, and then choose **Modify, Transform**. Next, choose either **Scale** or **Rotate**. In both cases, handles will appear around the text. To scale, click and drag to achieve the desired effect.

The same handles appear for both the rotate and skew effects. To rotate, click and drag one of the four corner boxes. To skew, click and drag on one of the side handles.

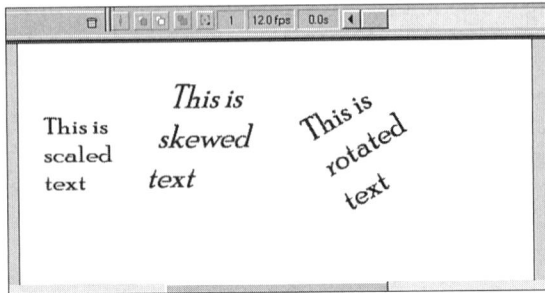

FIGURE 10.4
Examples of three effects that can be used on text. All three of these text blocks started out identical.

TIP

> You can apply superscript (writing above the main text line) or subscript (writing below the main text line) to selected letters. First, select the text you want to change. Then, open the **Character Panel** by choosing **Window, Panels, Character**. Choose either **Superscript** or **Subscript** from the drop-down menu. Figure 10.5 shows the menu, and highlights some superscripted text.

Flash 5 enables you to control attributes such as line spacing and alignment for paragraphs. Open the **Paragraph** dialog box by selecting **Window, Panels, Paragraph**. The boxes to the right of the word align enable you to align left, center, right, or full justified. See Figure 10.6 to view the **Paragraph** panel.

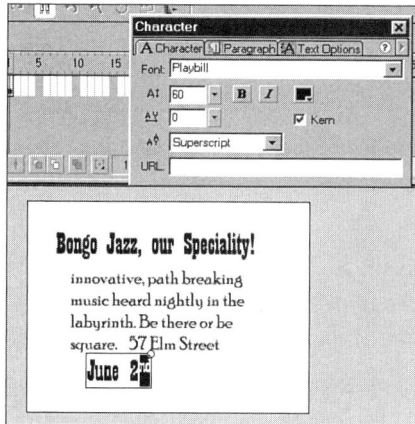

FIGURE 10.5

Superscript elevates the text above the main text line, and uses a smaller size font. The Superscript selection is made in the Character Panel.

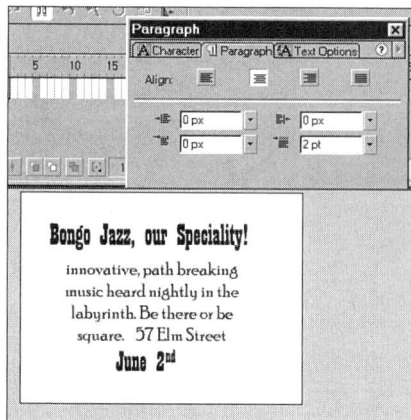

FIGURE 10.6

The Paragraph Panel. The center alignment box is highlighted, and the selected text has been centered.

TEXT TO SHAPE

Sometimes text won't appear the way you want when other people run it in their browsers. This is because other computers may not have the fonts you have applied to the text when creating it in Flash 5. Converting text to shapes ensures you that the text will appear exactly as you created it.

To convert text to shapes, first select the desired text box. Then choose **Modify**, **Break Apart** from the menu. Every letter is now a discrete shape. This enables you to apply all kinds of changes to your text.

You can change colors, skew it, rotate it, scale it, and apply other changes you would to any Flash object, and be certain that it will display in a browser the way you want. Figure 10.7 shows text that has been converted to shape and altered.

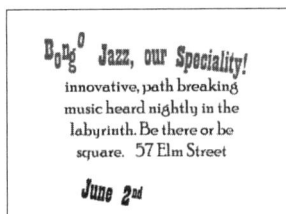

FIGURE 10.7
Converting text to shape enables you to manipulate it, and ensures that it will appear in a browser as you want.

TIP

Converted text takes up a lot more file space than ordinary Flash text. It's a good idea to use this effect when and where you need it.

Lesson 11
Making Symbols

In this lesson, you will learn to make reusable images called symbols,
to put symbols in Flash movies, and to customize symbols.

Creating Symbols

Symbols are images used repeatedly throughout your movie. There are
two great advantages to symbols: They reduce file size, and they are
easier to use than graphic objects. This means they will download and
stream much more quickly for people viewing your movie, and also
be easier for you to work with in creating your movie.

To create a new symbol, select **Insert**, **New Symbol**. The **Symbol
Properties** dialog box, shown in Figure 11.1, appears.

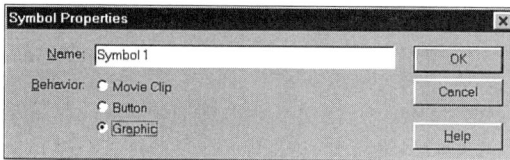

FIGURE 11.1
*The Symbol Properties dialog box allows you to give a name to your symbol, and
to select what type of symbol it is.*

TIP

> Develop a good and comprehensible naming system for
> your symbols, so you can keep track of them easily as
> they grow in numbers.

Specify the type of symbol you want by clicking in the appropriate option button. **Graphic** symbols are the most common. They consist of one static, in other words, nonanimated, frame. **Movie Clip** symbols, which are animated, and **Button** symbols, which perform a function when they are clicked, will be covered more fully in Lesson 14.

When you click OK, notice that a symbol icon appears above the Layers list next to the Scene Tab. This means you are editing a Symbol. Symbols are drawn and created like other Flash images. When you finish editing a Symbol, return to the regular mode by selecting **Edit, Edit Movie**.

Existing images can be converted to Symbols. Select all the objects you want to convert to a Symbol, keeping in mind that outlines are usually separate objects. Then, choose **Insert, Convert to Symbol**. The Symbol dialog box appears, and you proceed as with creating a new symbol. Figure 11.2 shows an image being converted to a Symbol.

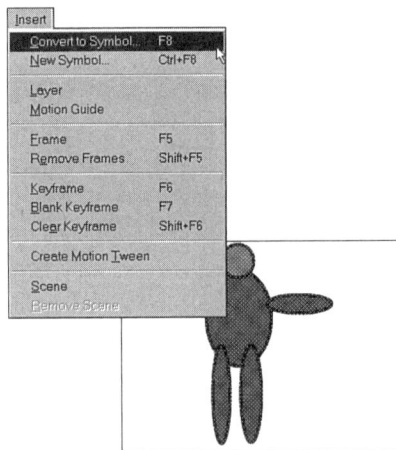

FIGURE 11.2
Converting an object to a Symbol. Make certain all the objects you want to become part of the Symbol are selected when you do this.

PUTTING SYMBOLS IN MOVIES

Symbols can be used over and over throughout a movie. They are stored in Libraries—which you will learn more about in the next lesson. But you can see symbols you have created for a particular movie as you work. Select **Window**, **Library** to open the Library for your movie.

When in the Library window, if you click on the lines of different symbols in your movie, an image of the symbol will appear in the white panel area at the top of the box. See Figure 11.3 for an example.

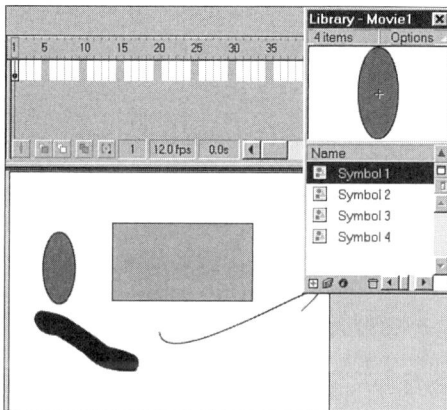

FIGURE 11.3
When a symbol line is clicked in a Library, an image of that symbol appears in the top panel of the dialog box.

CAUTION

Resist the temptation to use the Copy or Cut and Paste method of using images repeatedly in Flash. You will lose two of the main benefits of symbols: conserving file space and being able to edit a drawing throughout an entire movie.

To bring the desired symbol onto the stage, click and drag the symbol image to position it where you want. The symbol will remain in the Library, thus enabling you to use the same image repeatedly throughout your movie. As you create or convert more symbols than fit in the view panel of the dialog box, you can scroll through the box to get to all of them.

TIP

When many objects appear on your stage, it can sometimes be difficult to tell what is a Symbol and what isn't. To determine the difference, select the image. A Symbol will have a box around it and crosshairs in the middle and a Flash object will appear faded. Figure 11.4 shows two similar objects, one a Symbol and one not.

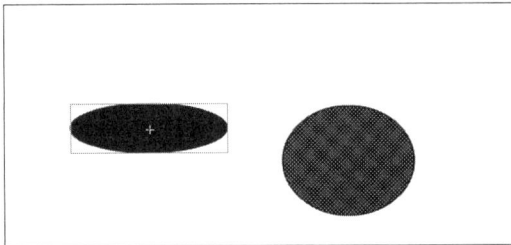

FIGURE 11.4
The oval on the left is a Symbol; the oval on the right is not.

EDITING SYMBOLS

Even after a Symbol is used multiple times in your movie, it can be edited globally. That is, it can be changed once so that its appearance changes, meaning each time it is displayed it has the changed look.

To edit a Symbol:

1. Click on the Symbol name in the Symbol Library window.

2. Next, double-click on the image in the top box of the window.

3. With the Symbol open, you can edit and transform it using the tools discussed in earlier lessons. It can be recolored, rotated, skewed, filled, or manipulated with any of the other tools and effects you learned.

4. When you have edited as you like, choose **Edit, Edit Movie**. This will return you to the movie on which you are working. The appearance of the Symbol in the box will have changed, as will the appearance of the Symbol every time it is shown in your movie.

You can also edit some of the particular attributes of an individual Symbol appearance, or what Flash calls an Instance. When a single Instance is edited, the changes are not applied globally. Only the appearance of the Symbol in that Instance changes.

NOTE

When you finish editing a symbol and return to regular editing mode, the Symbol you just made will not be visible on the stage. However, it will be stored in the Library and can be selected from the Library and placed on the Stage.

Symbol Instances can be rotated, scaled, skewed, and moved on the Stage. This means that if you apply these effects to one Instance of a Symbol, it will not impact the rest of your movie in any way. Figure 11.5 shows a Symbol that has been placed on the stage, and rotated.

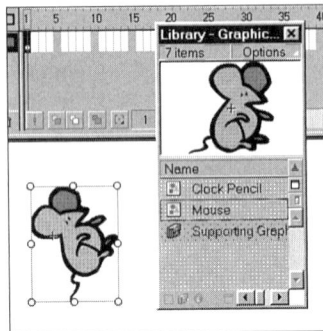

FIGURE 11.5

Single Instances of Symbols can be changed in some ways without impacting the Symbol's appearance elsewhere. Here a Symbol has been dragged onto the Stage and rotated.

Some changes cannot be made to Instances. These include fill changes using either the **Ink Bottle** or **Paint Bucket** tools.

It is possible to change the fill color of a Symbol Instance.

1. Select the Instance on the Stage.

2. Choose **Window, Panels, Effect**. This opens the **Effect Panel**.

3. Select **Tint** from the drop-down menu. Figure 11.6 shows the **Effect Panel** with **Tint** about to be selected.

Select a new color for the Instance from the palette or the mixer at the bottom of the screen. Other changes can be made through the **Effect Panel**, including changing using the **Brightness** option to make the color of the symbol lighter or darker, and the **Alpha** option to make it more or less transparent.

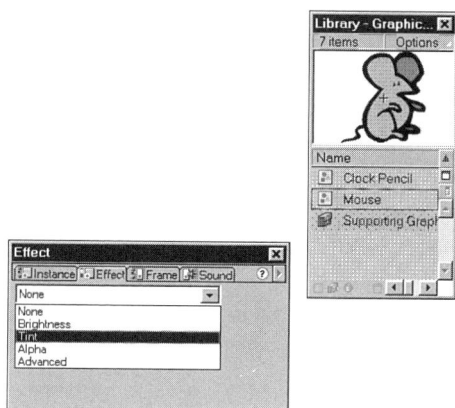

FIGURE 11.6
The color of a single Symbol Instance can be changed through the Effect Panel.

LESSON 12
Organizing with Libraries

In this lesson, you will learn how to use Flash 5 libraries to organize and keep track of your Symbols.

THE SYMBOL LIBRARY

You can quickly amass a large collection of Symbols when you are designing a movie for Flash 5. Developing a good naming and filing system for your Symbols is essential to help keep them organized and recognizable by you.

Flash 5 Libraries help you control and organize your Symbols.

When you start a Flash 5 movie, one main Library is created for it. This Library is where the material created or deposited (imported for use) in that particular movie is held.

To see that Library, select **Window, Library**. Figure 12.1 shows the **Library** selection being made.

The Symbol Library opens with a small panel. But it can be enlarged to provide you with a better view of the information it contains. To enlarge the panel, click and drag one of its edges to get to the desired size, or simply click the button located to the right of the first Library listing.

The Wide view of the Library gives detailed information on the Library contents. It lets you know the name of each Symbol, what kind of Symbol it is, how many times it's been used in your movie, and the last time it was modified. Figure 12.2 shows a view of a Library dialog box in Wide view.

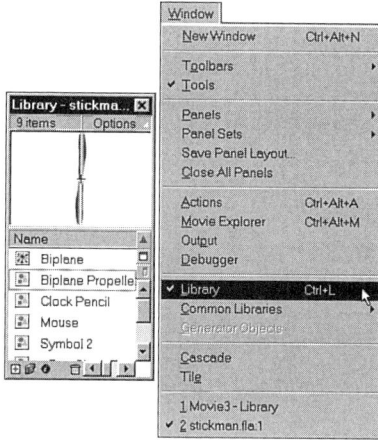

FIGURE 12.1

Selecting the Library from the toolbar. The Library panel is open here and a selection has been made from it. Also, one Symbol from the library has been dragged on the Stage and is partially visible.

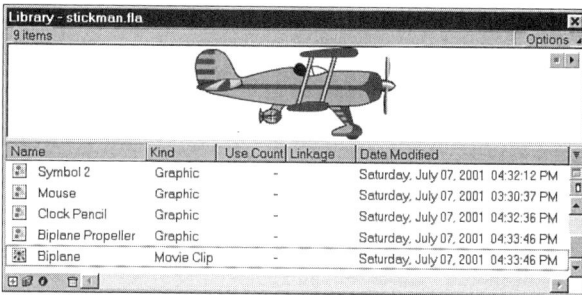

FIGURE 12.2

The Library dialog box in Wide View. Detailed information is provided for all the Symbols in a Library.

NEW TERM

The **Linkage** column in the Library panel indicates whether a symbol is linked with a Web location.

TIP

> Flash keeps track of how many times a Symbol is used only if you tell it to. To do this, open the **Options** selection in the Library dialog box by clicking on the arrow beneath the X in the upper-right corner. Then, make sure the **Keep Use Counts Updated** option is checked. Figure 12.3 shows the **Options** menu opened.

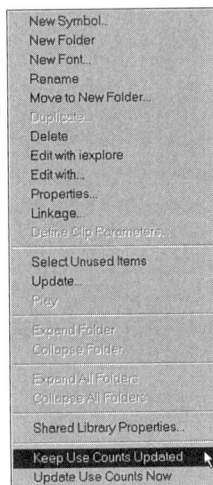

FIGURE 12.3
Checking the Keep Use Counts Updated selection enables you to track how many times a Symbol is used in your movie.

It is helpful to create enough folders in a Library to accommodate all your Symbols. To create a new folder, again open the **Options** selections, and choose **New Folder**. Another method is simply to click the folder icon at the bottom of the dialog box.

After you have the new folder, click and drag Symbols to it within the dialog box. Figure 12.4 shows a folder open in Wide view.

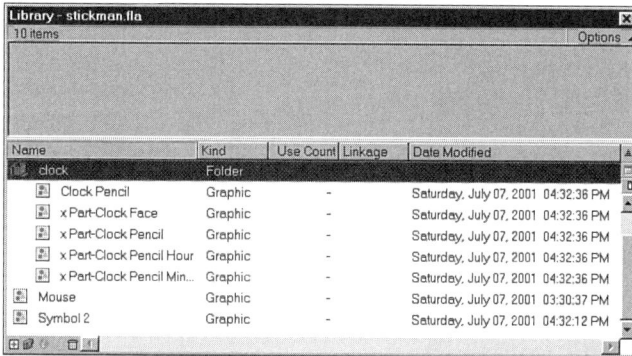

FIGURE 12.4

An open folder in the Library dialog box. Flash movies can accumulate dozens, even hundreds of Symbols, and it is important to develop good methods of organizing them.

TIP

One of the most helpful choices in the **Options** box is **Duplicate**. This enables you to create a new Symbol that is identical to the one selected. You can then edit the new one so that it is similar to, but somewhat different from, the original. The original Symbol can still be used as desired.

To delete a Symbol, select the Symbol you want to delete in the Library dialog box; then select **Delete** from the options window. You can also select the Symbol to be deleted and then click the trash can icon at the bottom of the panel. A warning will appear, as shown in Figure 12.5.

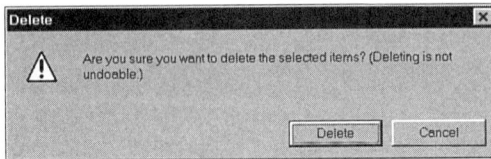

FIGURE 12.5
A warning appears before a Symbol is deleted from a Library.

SHARING LIBRARIES

Entire libraries created for one movie can be utilized in other movies. This can greatly enhance the number of symbols you can draw upon to create movies as you continue to use Flash 5. To utilize a library external to your movie, select **File, Open As Library** from the toolbar. Double-click the movie whose Library you want to open, or highlight that movie name and click **Open**. The Library will be imported to your current movie. Figure 12.6 shows the **Open As Library** box.

Shared Libraries are a new feature in Flash 5. Symbols you will use in several movies, perhaps a logo or particular Text image, can be stored in a Library and used in multiple projects. To use symbols from a shared Library, choose **File, Open As Shared Library**. Locate the movie whose Library you want to share, and open it as in the preceding step.

TIP

Shared Libraries can be valuable timesavers. To maximize their utility, you may find it best to place your shared Library movies in folders and files that are clearly marked and readily recognized. You can even create a folder used only for shared Libraries. Create a new folder and store the FLA files you intend to use repeatedly in it.

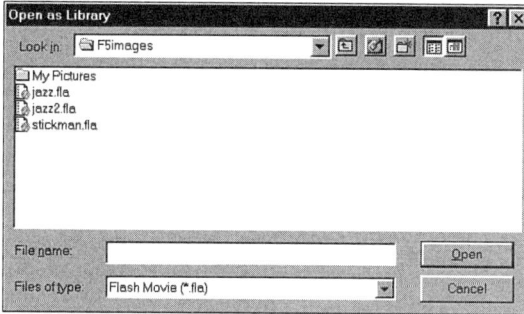

FIGURE 12.6
Libraries and Symbols created for one Flash movie can be used in other movies.

Learning to manage Libraries well is a key part of developing mastery of Flash. Try to organize your Symbols and Libraries with names and in an order that makes sense to you, and serves the movie you are creating. And keep in mind that you can reorganize as you go along. Often, time spent reorganizing the Library (or Libraries) for a movie will be productive and save you time overall.

LESSON 13
Frame by Frame Animation

In this lesson, you will learn the basics of how Flash 5 animation works. You will learn to define Frames for Animation, and to use Symbols for animation.

THE TIMELINE AND FLASH ANIMATION

Animation is the heart of why people use Flash. The Timeline you were introduced to earlier in the book is a key part of developing Flash animation.

Flash animation works by playing through the Timeline. Each numbered Frame in the Timeline can be composed of multiple layers. Thus, at any point in the playback, the total appearance on the computer screen is the set of layers designed for that particular frame.

The Flash Timeline has horizontal and vertical gradations. The horizontal gradations indicate the Frames. The number of Frames in your movie's Timeline will correspond to the length of the movie. The vertical gradations indicate the Layers within particular Frames.

> **NEW TERM**
>
> **Gradations** are the steps of measurement into which a scale is broken.

Figure 13.1 shows the Flash Timeline.

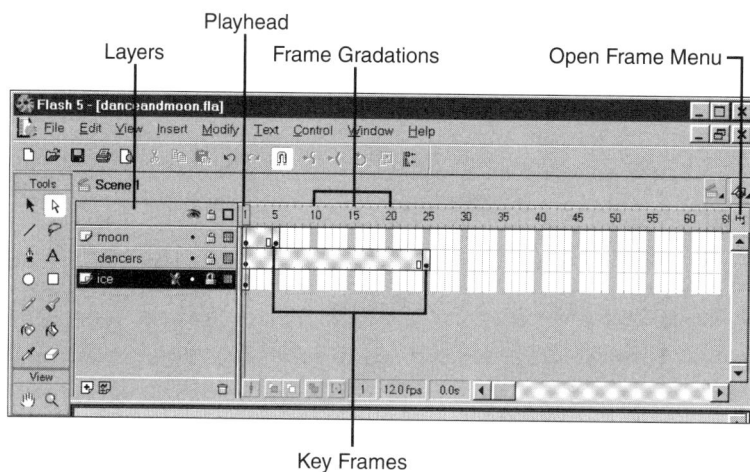

Playhead
Layers   Frame Gradations   Open Frame Menu

Key Frames

FIGURE 13.1

The Flash Timeline keeps track of Frames in the horizontal bar, and Layers in each Frame in the vertical bar.

The Timeline is graduated into units of five. The Playhead—the red box with a line running down out of it—indicates the Frame in which you are working. In a new movie, in which there is only one Frame, you cannot move the Playhead.

TIP

> The Playhead provides an important tool for moving to any Frame in your movie. You can either drag it back and forth to get to the desired Frame, or click the Frame you want. In either case, you will get a view of how your movie looks in that Frame.

The arrow to the right of the Timeline opens a menu that enables you to change the appearance of your Timeline. Some of the options here enable you to enlarge or reduce the size of the Timeline.

Another helpful option enables you to view thumbnail sketches of the contents of each Frame. These are **Preview** and **Preview in Context**. Figure 13.2 shows the menu open with the **Preview** box checked.

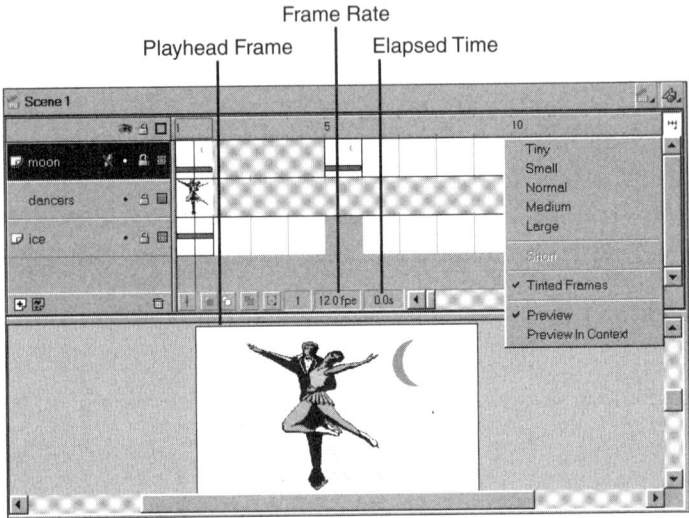

FIGURE 13.2
The menu at the right of the Timeline enables you to change how the Timeline looks. With the Preview box checked, a thumbnail image of the selected Frame appears in the Timeline.

There are three numbered values on the bottom of the Timeline. They all define important time values of a movie. The first tells the frame on which the Playhead is located. The second tells Frame Rate, measured in frames per second. The third tells total elapsed time.

TIP

It is helpful to experiment, and learn to manage the Frame Rate properly. Too high a Frame Rate means a blurry movie. Too low means very little animation effect. A good standard to start with is generally around 12 frames per second.

DEFINE FRAMES FOR ANIMATION

As you create a Flash 5 movie, the Timeline distinguishes between frames that are empty and those with content. Before Frames have any content, they appear as empty, blank boxes, each separated by a solid line. The appearance changes when a Frame is occupied. The area under the Timeline numbers becomes gray, and the solid line between boxes is no longer there.

Certain Frames, called Keyframes, represent events and changes in the movie animation. You will learn more about Keyframes in Lesson 16, "Animating with Keyframes." But they can be recognized on the timeline by a black dot on one side of a vertical line running through the timeline.

The dot represents the appearance of an object or event on the Stage. The small rectangle to the left of this line represents the end of an event or object on the Stage. Therefore, when an animation begins travelling through the Timeline, changes in its appearance will occur in these marked Frames, or Keyframes. Figure 13.3 shows a Timeline with several Keyframes.

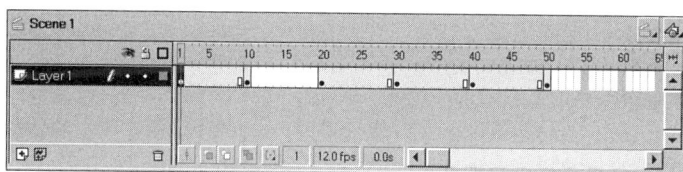

FIGURE 13.3
The Timeline indicates Frames that are Keyframes, Frames that are empty, and Frames that are occupied. There are six Keyframes in this image.

When you select **File**, **New**, you start with a set of frames for your movie. If you just create an object (or objects) using your drawing tools, or select a Symbol you have stored in a Library and drag it on Stage, it will be allotted to a Frame.

You select another Keyframe by clicking on the desired number in the Timeline and pressing **F6** on the keyboard. Animation in Flash 5 is the craft of defining the movement between these Frames. The movement of an image introduced in one Keyframe will end or change in the next. Figure 13.4 shows the beginning of a simple animation—movement of a Symbol through the Timeline.

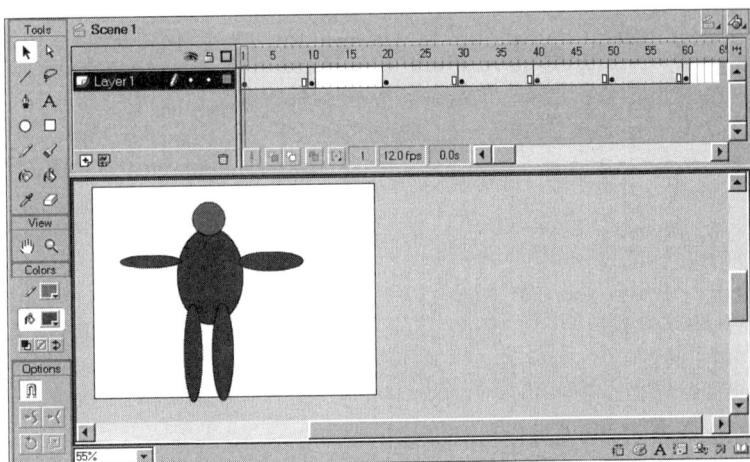

FIGURE 13.4
The beginning of a simple animation before it begins to move through the Timeline.

You can see what your animation will look like at any Keyframe point in the Timeline by clicking on that Frame. Figure 13.5 shows the same image—a Symbol—at Frame 30.

The same process of selecting a Frame and clicking **F6** can be utilized repeatedly to set Keyframes at whatever intervals you want. To see how your animation works between any Keyframes, simply select the first Keyframe and press **Enter**.

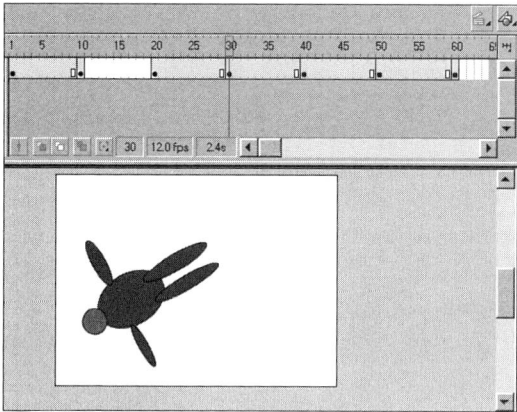

FIGURE 13.5

The same movie at Frame 30. The Symbol used in the opening Frame has been reduced and rotated.

TIP

> Avoid the temptation to make every Frame into a
> Keyframe. As you learn more about animation, you will
> learn how to develop changes determined in Keyframes
> into a smooth, seamless presentation. Where to place
> Keyframes is an art that will grow as your familiarity
> with Flash and its possibilities grows.

LESSON 14
Making Interactive Buttons

In this lesson, you will learn how Flash buttons work, how to use Flash library buttons, how to create buttons, and how to define areas for buttons.

UNDERSTANDING FLASH BUTTONS

Buttons are essential to Flash's interactivity. Buttons are objects that react when a mouse comes in contact with them. They enable the viewer of a Flash site to enter or leave portions of the site, to begin movies or audio clips, to jump to a desired area of the Flash movie, and to perform other functions.

There are four states for each Button: **Up**, **Over**, **Down**, and **Hit** (see Table 14.1).

NEW TERM

A button **state** describes the appearance of a button at different phases of its interaction with the visitor using his or her mouse.

TABLE 14.1 Four States of Buttons

Button	State of Button
Up	The button before it is clicked.
Over	How the button looks when the cursor hovers over it.
Down	How the button looks when it is clicked.
Hit	The area assigned or defined to respond to the mouse action, such as clicking or hovering.

Figure 14.1 shows the same Web site you saw in Lesson 1, "Meet Flash 5." Each of the dates on the left of the page is a Button that activates information on the right side of the page when the cursor hovers over the date.

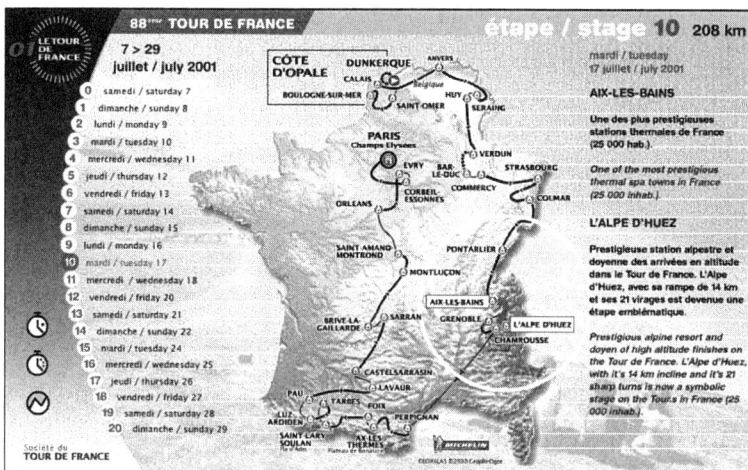

FIGURE 14.1
The dates on the left act as Buttons in this site. When the mouse hovers over the various Buttons, information about that date flashes up on the right side of the page.

Button Libraries

Flash 5 has an ample selection of clip art buttons in its Button Library. Select **Window, Common Libraries, Buttons** to find the premade buttons. Double-click a button folder to see the folder's contents. With a folder open, click a button name beneath it to see a sample of that button displayed in the window. Figure 14.2 shows an example of a button in the Library window.

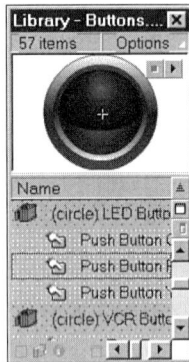

FIGURE 14.2
You can browse the selection of Buttons in the Flash 5 Library, and view them before placing them on your stage.

To put the Library button on the stage, click and drag to place it where you want. You can see what the button will look like in its different states by selecting **Control, Enable Simple Buttons**. The button will display differently when you hover over it or click it with your mouse.

When the button is on the stage, it can be manipulated with rotation, skewing, and other effects, as described in Lesson 6, "Selecting and Manipulating Objects." Text often clarifies a button's function for visitors to your site. Some buttons in the Flash library come with text, but you can also place text on or near your button, using the same methods described in Lesson 10, "Adding Text to a Movie." However, keep in mind that buttons can't be edited with the **Enable Simple Buttons** feature selected.

CAUTION

It's important to test your buttons and see how they look in different modes. But when you are finished testing, it usually is best to disable the **Enable Simple Buttons** command. It can get confusing and distracting if you are working on other portions of your frame or layer with this feature activated.

CREATE A BUTTON

To create a new Button, select **Insert**, **New Symbol** from the toolbar. In the **Symbol Properties** dialog box, click Button, and enter a name for your Button. Click **OK** when finished. Figure 14.3 shows a new button being made.

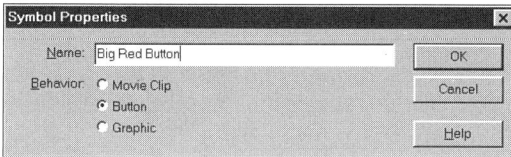

FIGURE 14.3
Create and name Buttons by selecting the New Symbol option in the dialog box.

The name of your Button then appears above the Timeline. Just below the Button name are frames with the four Button states marked.

TIP

> It is helpful to develop a naming system for your buttons that will make sense to you as you get deeper into the development of a Flash 5 project.

After clicking **OK**, draw and edit the button symbol to make it the way you want. The completed shape will be the Up state of your new button. Add the Over state of the button by clicking in the **Over** frame. Then select either **Insert**, **Keyframe**, which will duplicate the previous frame with the Up state of the button in the new frame, or **Insert**, **Blank Keyframe**, which will enable you to draw a new button shape for the Over state. In both cases, edit the button to achieve the effect you desire. Figure 14.4 shows the Over state selected for button creation.

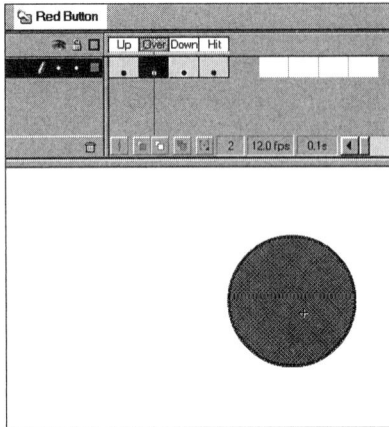

FIGURE 14.4
When you make your own buttons, you design each state of the button.

Design the **Down** state using the same method used to create the **Over** state.

The **Hit** State is somewhat different from the other three states. It defines the area on which a mouse click activates a button. Create the **Hit** state by selecting the Hit frame, again selecting either **Insert**, **Keyframe** or **Insert**, **Blank Keyframe**, and then drawing a shape that will be the clickable area of the button.

Buttons can be tested by selecting **Control**, **Test Movie**, or **Control**, **Enable Simple Buttons**. Figure 14.5 shows a button being tested using the **Test Movie** option.

TIP

The image you place in the **Hit** state is invisible in the movie. You just need a solid area of adequate size to respond to the mouse. It doesn't need to be the exact size of the button—in fact, sometimes an area slightly larger than the button is helpful.

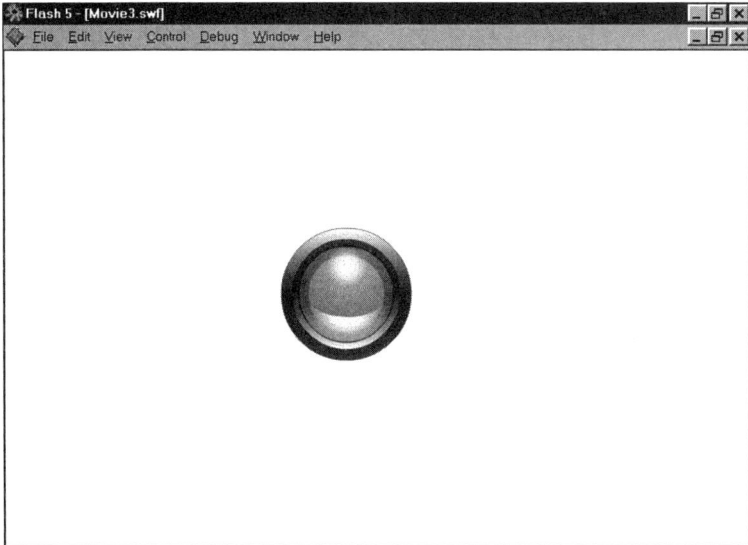

FIGURE 14.5
*Testing a button in **Test Movie** mode. The image here is in the **Hit** state, and the Hit area is larger than the button. To return to your Flash 5 stage, click the Close button (X) in the Test window.*

When you have finished editing a button, return to normal editing by selecting **Edit**, **Edit Movie**.

Lesson 15

Assigning Actions to Buttons

In this lesson, you will learn how to assign actions to Flash 5 buttons. You will learn how to use buttons to stop the action in a movie, to move to other scenes in your movie, and to move to other Web pages.

MOUSE EVENTS

To be functional, buttons need actions, such as stopping and starting the movie, jumping to another scene, or linking to another Web page assigned to them. The first step in assigning action is to determine the event that will trigger the action.

With a button on the stage (either one that you designed or one from the Flash Button Library), first select the button with the **Arrow** tool. Then, choose **Modify, Instance** from the menu bar. Click the **Edit Actions** icon in the lower-right corner of the panel to open the **Object Actions** panel. In this panel, click **Basic Actions** to display Actions options, and select **On Mouse Event**. Figure 15.1 shows the **On Mouse Event** selection being made.

NEW TERM

> **Mouse Event**: The awkward phrase "Mouse Event" refers to the actions a site visitor takes with their mouse, such as clicking or hovering.

Double-click the **On Mouse Event** selection to open the Option window for mouse events. Figure 15.2 shows the **On Mouse Events** Options Window open.

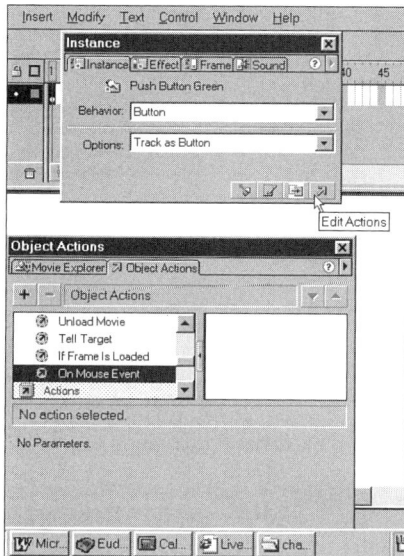

FIGURE 15.1

*In this figure, a button has been placed on the stage, and panels have been opened to assign actions to it. Clicking the **Edit Actions** icon opens the **Object Actions** panel.*

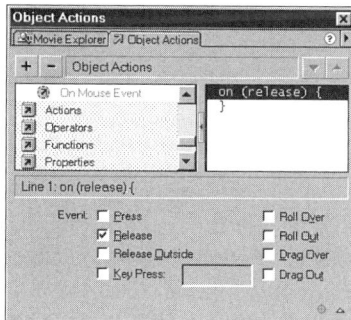

FIGURE 15.2

Choosing a mouse event.

Table 15.1 shows possible mouse events.

TABLE 15.1   Mouse Events

Mouse Event	Description
Press	Clicking on the mouse initiates the action.
Release	The action begins when the mouse button is clicked and released.
Release Outside	Clicking and then moving outside the Hit frame begins the action.
Key Press	Event is triggered when a key is pressed.
Roll Over	The event begins when the visitor hovers over the button without clicking.
Roll Out	The option begins when the mouse cursor moves over and then off a button without clicking.
Drag Over	The action is triggered when a visitor clicks the button, and drags the cursor off the button and then back on again.
Drag Out	The action is triggered by clicking the button and dragging the cursor off the button.

When you have selected the mouse event, Flash 5 generates Action Script code in the box of the **Object Actions** panel.

NEW TERM

Action Script is the computer programming language used by Flash. You can eventually learn to create your own names for Flash functions and define them in Action Script, but Flash enables you to utilize this powerful tool while learning little, or even nothing, of the actual coding. Action Script is what enables Flash to be responsive and interactive.

TIP

> More than one event can be assigned to a button. But it's best to keep things simple, and assign only one. It's also best to keep your events limited to **Press**, **Release**, and **Roll Over**.

STOP ACTION, URLS, AND JUMPING TO NEW SCENES

The other step in defining action is to determine the action assigned to the button. Buttons can stop and start the playing of the movie, jump to particular scenes, and go to Web site locations. Figure 15.3 shows a frame with buttons taken from the button library. Text has been added near the buttons to explain the actions the buttons initiate.

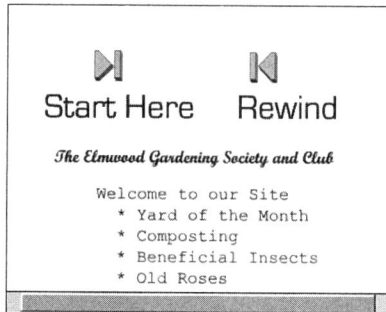

FIGURE 15.3
Flash libraries provide buttons that intuitively help visitors understand how to view the movie.

Assign a start action to a button by selecting **Window, Actions**. This is another way of opening the **Object Options** panel. Click the + sign in the panel, select **Basic Actions**, and then click **On Mouse Event**. Figure 15.4 shows the **Basic Actions** menu opened.

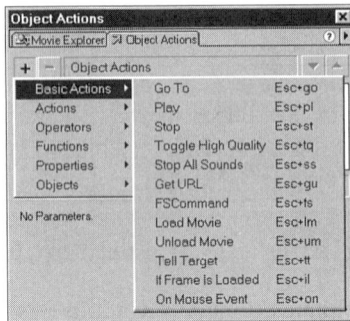

FIGURE 15.4
The Basic Actions menu is used to assign actions to buttons.

After you choose the mouse event you want to trigger the action, click the + icon again. Choose **Basic Actions**, **Play** from the list of menu options. Click **OK** to close the panel.

To add a Stop button on a page, follow the same steps, but select **Stop** instead of **Play.** You can test the buttons by selecting **Control**, **Test Movie**. Hover over and click the buttons to see whether they are working.

You can also make your button trigger a leap to another Web site. To do this, again open the **Object Actions** panel by selecting **Window**, **Action**. Open the menu by clicking on the +, but this time choose **Basic Actions**, **Get URL**. Type in the address of the URL (Uniform Resource Locator), making sure to include the http://. Figure 15.5 shows an URL button being added to a page.

Test an URL button by selecting **File**, **Publish Preview**, **Default**. Your movie will now open in a browser, and you can test the button's operations. If you are connected to the Internet, the mouse event on your button should link you to the desired site.

You can also configure buttons so that visitors can go to particular frames or scenes in your movie. This can be particularly helpful as people come back to your site repeatedly, and probably won't want to be viewing the entire movie each time.

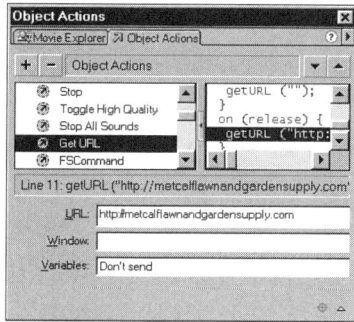

FIGURE 15.5
Flash buttons can be linked to other Web sites.

To allow visitors to go to particular frames, select **Window**, **Actions**. Click the + icon and again select **Basic Actions**, **On Mouse Event**. After selecting the mouse event you want, make sure it is highlighted in the right side of the panel and again click the + sign. Now, select **Basic Actions**, **Go To**. Figure 15.6 shows the **Go To** option highlighted in the **Object Actions** panel.

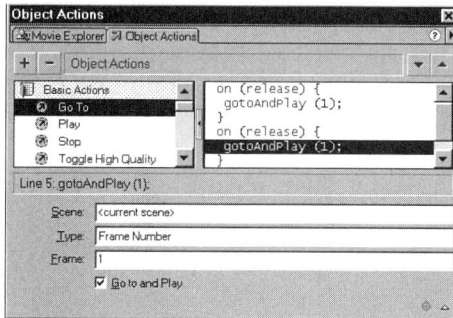

FIGURE 15.6
You can configure buttons to allow visitors to jump to particular frames or scenes in your movie.

Enter a target frame number in the **Frame Number** area of the panel to go to a particular frame. If your movie has more than one scene, you can choose another scene by entering it in the panel space or choosing it from the Scene drop-down menu.

LESSON 16

Animating with Keyframes

In this lesson, you will learn about Keyframes, and be introduced to the basics of video and text animation.

UNDERSTANDING KEYFRAMES

Animation is the heart of Flash, and Keyframes are at the heart of how the animation works. Flash has two types of animation, frame by frame and "tweening." Frame by frame animation means the creator designs the content of each frame of the movie. The complex task of constructing multiframe animation can be broken down into the task of creating Keyframes.

Keyframes mark when action or events begin and end in the Timeline. When you open a file to create a new movie, a blank Keyframe is inserted in the first frame.

NEW TERM

There are three types of frames. **Keyframes** have content placed in them. **Static Frames** don't have their own content, but continue to display the content of the Keyframe that preceded them. **Blank Keyframes** don't display anything.

As indicated in Lesson 13, "Frame by Frame Animation," a Keyframe is marked on the Timeline with a black dot. In Figure 16.1, frames 1 and 20 are Keyframes.

FIGURE 16.1
Keyframes delineate action within Flash movies. This movie is in frame 1.

ADDING KEYFRAMES

Add a blank Keyframe to your movie by clicking the Timeline in the frame you want to make into a Keyframe. Then, choose **Insert, Blank Keyframe** from the toolbar. The blank Keyframe will not display the content of the previous Keyframe(s). Figures 16.2 and 16.3 show the second and third Keyframes of a simple movie. In the first, the content from the first Keyframe was moved and changed. In the second, it was again changed.

You can create a new Keyframe that displays images on the stage of the previous Keyframe. The contents of the new Keyframe can then be manipulated to achieve a different effect. In Figure 16.2, the airplane in Keyframe 1 was moved to a different location, old text was removed, and new text was added, using the same font and size.

Create a new nonblank Keyframe by clicking on the frame in which you want the Keyframe, and then selecting **Insert, Keyframe** from the toolbar, as shown in Figure 16.4.

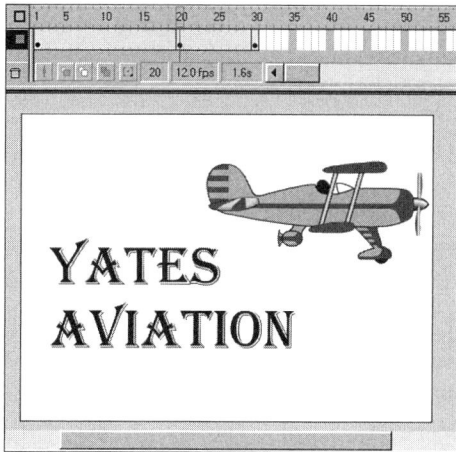

FIGURE 16.2
In the second Keyframe, the same symbol has been used, but it has been moved. New text appears, in a different stage location.

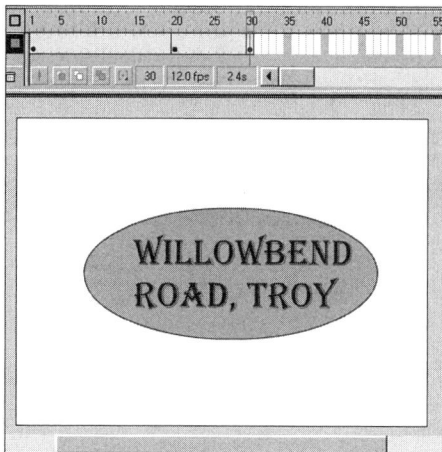

FIGURE 16.3
The third Keyframe was created by inserting a Blank Keyframe and creating new content. When the movie plays, it will go through all three Keyframes.

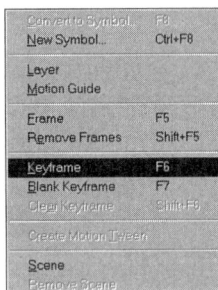

FIGURE 16.4
*Content in one Keyframe can reappear and be manipulated in another by selecting **Insert, Keyframe**.*

DELETING, CLEARING, AND MOVING KEYFRAMES

Keyframes can be cleared and deleted. Clear a Keyframe when you don't want a change to occur in that specific frame. Clear by right-clicking the Keyframe and selecting **Clear Keyframe**. This frame now becomes an ordinary frame. To delete a Keyframe, right-click the selected frame and choose **Remove Frames**.

You can select and move Keyframes backward and forward in the Timeline. First, click the Keyframe dot in the Timeline. When you select a Keyframe in this way, the dot changes from black to white, and the Stage contents are selected. Then, click the dot and drag forward or backward to the desired Timeline location.

CAUTION

Keyframes have some idiosyncrasies. Choosing **Delete Frame** when you are on a Keyframe other than the last frame of a layer will cause Flash to remove one frame from your movie, but it won't be the Keyframe. To clear such a Keyframe, first choose **Clear Keyframe** and then delete the frame in a separate, distinct action.

You can determine how the content of different Keyframes appears in relation to one another by clicking the **Onion Skin** option. Figure 16.5 shows how to activate Onion Skin. Onion skinning makes frames in a layer semitransparent. This enables you to see and place objects in relation to their position in different frames.

TIP

> Onion skinning is especially helpful when you are creating buttons, and developing the size of the hit frame in relation to other button frames.

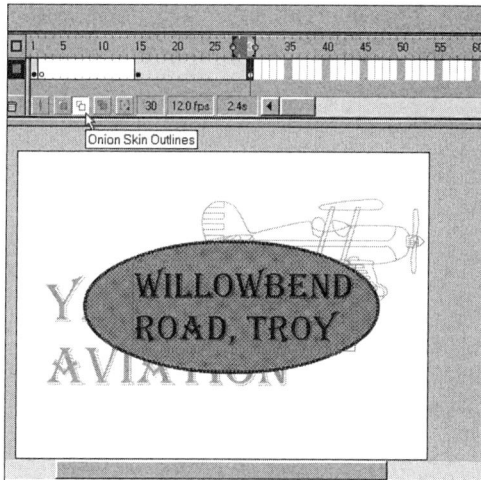

FIGURE 16.5
The onion skinning option is a form of semitransparency that enables you to see objects in different frames in outline form.

TESTING YOUR MOVIE

You can test your movie by selecting **Control, Play** from the menu. Bring it back to the first Keyframe by selecting **Control, Rewind**. To see how your movie looks in the Flash Viewer, select **Control**, **Test Movie**.

You can also go through a frame-by-frame test of your movie. Select **Window**, **Toolbars**, **Controller** to see the Control window. Figure 16.6 shows the Control window, which has keys similar to those on video or tape players. Click the keys to play the movie in the desired direction.

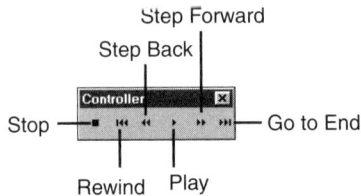

FIGURE 16.6
The Control Window enables you to view your movie frame by frame.

You can speed up or slow down the play of your movie. Select **Modify**, **Movie**, and the **Movie Properties** dialog box appears. The Frame Rate box determines the speed with which your movie plays. Slower speeds can make the movie seem more like a series of slides. You can experiment with different speeds, but 12fps (frames per second) is the norm. Change the speed by changing the value in the frame rate box. Figure 16.7 shows the **Movie Properties** dialog box.

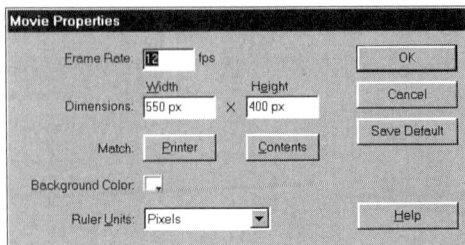

FIGURE 16.7
*The **Movie Properties** dialog box allows you to adjust the speed at which a movie plays.*

TIP

Many factors go into determining appropriate frame rate. Too high a frame rate can result in a low visual effect, as the frames fly by too quickly to view. A high frame rate also means you must create more frames for your movie. Sometimes a movie that's large at particular points can be adjusted by speeding up the frame rate. But movies will play differently in different computers with different processors. Along with experimenting to get the best result, keep in mind the audience you are aiming for with your movie.

LESSON 17
Flowing Animation

In this lesson, you will learn to create smooth, flowing animation with a process called tweening.

UNDERSTANDING TWEENING

Animation in Flash can be made smooth and flowing without performing the tedious and time-consuming task of creating thousands of frames, each with tiny differences from those preceding and following it.

The technique called tweening—so named because it transforms the properties of elements between Keyframes—enables your animations to become more complex and pleasant to the viewer.

When you tween your animation, you start by creating the artwork for the first frame of the tweened sequence. Then, you add a Keyframe for the final frame of the sequence. Flash generates all the frames in between through the tweening process.

Tweening takes up considerably less file space than frame by frame animation. Flash doesn't need to store the values for each frame as it is tweened, only for the changes being made between frames.

There are two types of tweening. *Motion* tween changes properties of a symbol, such as its position, color, shape, or size. *Shape* tween transforms one shape into another.

> **TIP**
>
> Motion tweening works only on symbols. It will not work on an image you have just drawn on the stage.

Before moving on to tweening, you may find it helpful to review the basics of layers, symbols, frames, and the Timeline. The process of tweening itself is relatively straightforward and simple. But many of the aspects of Flash about which you've been learning come to bear when you begin to tween your animations.

MOTION TWEENING

Key to any sequence of motion tweening are its start and end points. Put a symbol on the first frame of your Timeline. Next select the frame in which you want the sequence to end. Convert this frame to a Keyframe by selecting **Insert, Keyframe**, or simply pressing the **F6** key, and move the symbol to a different point on the stage.

Right-click in a frame between the two selected frames and choose **Create Motion Tween**. Figure 17.1 shows the **Create Motion Tween** selection being made.

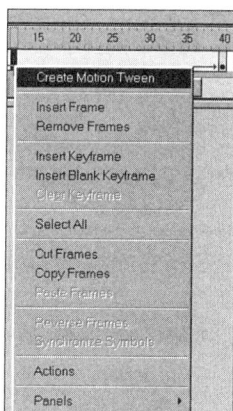

FIGURE 17.1
The Create Motion Tween selection smooths the flow of symbols between frames.

The tweened frames turn blue and an arrow connects the area between the two Keyframes when you tween. Figure 17.2 shows a section of a Timeline to which tweening has been applied.

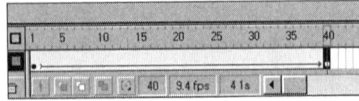

FIGURE 17.2
In this figure, the arrow and blue coloring between frames 1 and 40 indicate that tweening has been applied to them.

Figures 17.3 and 17.4 show an example of a tweened animation at its beginning and end points. The skaters leap across the stage as the movie plays, and the text appears at the end of the sequence.

FIGURE 17.3
In this sequence, the skaters move smoothly across the stage.

Effects such as scaling and rotating can be applied to tweened images. Scaling to make an image grow larger can make the image seem to be moving toward the viewer as the movie plays.

FIGURE 17.4
The name of the rink appears in the last frame.

To scale a tween:

1. Click in the frame you want the scaling to begin and choose **Insert, Keyframe**.

2. After placing the symbol on the stage, click the frame you want to end the scaling effect, and again choose **Insert, Keyframe**.

3. Select the object you want to scale, and then choose **Modify, Transform, Scale** from the menu.

4. Handles appear around the object, which can now be scaled as you learned in a previous lesson.

5. Right-click in the frames between the two Keyframes and choose **Create Motion Tween**.

6. Test your movie by clicking the first Keyframe of the scaled sequence and selecting **Control, Test Movie**. Figures 17.5 and 17.6 show scaled tween that appears to be skating toward the viewer.

FIGURE 17.5
Effects such as scaling and rotating can be applied to tweened images.

FIGURE 17.6
Scaling makes an image appear to be approaching the viewer as it grows larger on the screen.

You can also change color in a tween sequence. Develop and select your beginning and ending Keyframes the same way you would to scale. Click in the final frame of the color changing sequence and open the effect panel by choosing **Window**, **Panels**, **Effect**. Choose the color property you want to change from the drop-down menu, or change the color entirely by selecting another one from the flyout menu. Click in the frames between the two Keyframes and select **Create Motion Tween,** and view the transformation as you have other tweened effects.

TIP

> You can apply more than one effect when tweening. For instance, changing colors and scaling can be combined.

You can also designate a path for objects to follow during a tweened sequence. A *motion guide* is a line that defines a path for your object to follow through the tweening. To create one, select the Keyframes and activate tweening between them as you would for other effects.

Then choose **Insert, Motion Guide** from the menu. When you do this, a new layer labeled Guide appears above your selected layer. Below it is the name of the layer to which the guide will be applied. In the guide layer, use the **Pencil, Line,** or **Pen tool** to draw a guide line for the tweened object's motion. Test as you would for other effects. Figure 17.7 shows a guideline and the object that follows it.

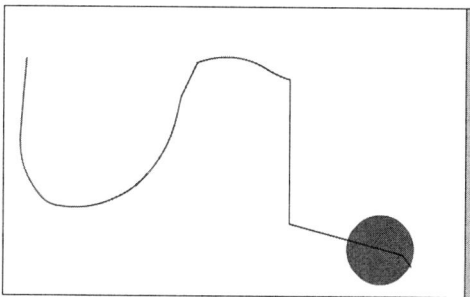

FIGURE 17.7
A tweened object can be made to follow a designated path. The guide line will not appear when the movie is seen in the Flash viewer.

Shape Tweening

Motion tweening changes the location of a symbol instance. Shape tweening changes the shape, by morphing between two faces. Unlike Motion tweens, Shape tweens are not made with symbols.

Shape tweens also start and end on Keyframes. Select the Keyframe you want to be the start of your Shape tween, and use any of the drawing tools to create an object. Click in the intended end frame, select **Insert**, **Blank Keyframe**, and draw what you intend the final shape to look like.

Select the frames between the two Keyframes, and choose **Modify, Frame** from the toolbar. The **Frame** panel, shown in Figure 17.8, will appear. Select **Shape** from the tween drop-down menu.

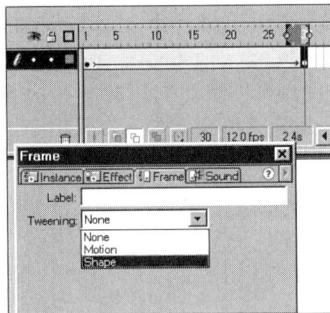

FIGURE 17.8
When a Shape tween is created, the selected frames will have a solid arrow running through green frames.

The **Blend** drop-down box contains two blending options when Shape tweening. **Angular** is best for shapes with sharp corners and angles; **Distributive** is best for smoother shapes. The **Easing** box enables you to determine the rate of tweening between Keyframes. Positive values slow down the rate as the tween nears the end Keyframe; negative values speed it up.

LESSON 18
Managing Animation

In this lesson, you will learn how to manage your movies through the use of scenes. You will also learn to create movie clips and animated symbols.

CREATING SCENES

Creating multiple scenes can be an important method of breaking up your movies. Scenes in Flash are roughly analogous to reels in a conventional movie. Effective use of scenes can make your movie easier to edit and develop, and can make it easier for visitors to view the parts they desire.

TIP

It often helps to organize your thoughts and, on paper, draw an outline of what you want your movie to look like. If you create a page that has several distinct components, such as Home Page, New Products, Service, and Locations, for example, you may want to break the movie into a scene for each of its subjects.

When you begin a new movie, by default it contains one scene. The name of the scene is above and to the left of the Timeline. Add a scene by choosing **Insert**, **Scene** from the menu, as shown in Figure 18.1.

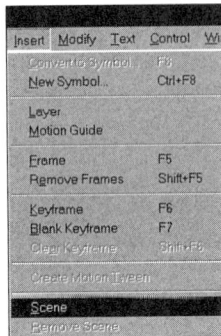

FIGURE 18.1
Inserting a scene from the Toolbar.

Scenes can also be added from the Scene Panel. Open this panel by choosing **Window, Panels, Scene**. Figure 18.2 shows the scene panel.

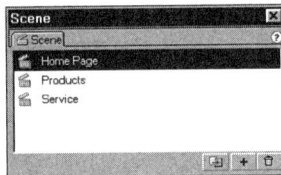

FIGURE 18.2
The Scene Panel enables you to manage control of many scenes.

You can change the name of a scene by double-clicking it in the Scene Panel, and typing in a new name. The name of the active scene is displayed above the Timeline.

The three icons at the bottom of the Scene Panel enable you to add a scene, delete a scene, and duplicate a scene. Duplication is helpful as a sort of template when creating a scene that has many elements in common with one already made.

When you test your movie by selecting **Control, Test Movie**, the scenes play in the order in which they are listed in the Scene Panel. If

you want to change the order, open the Scene Panel, click the scene
you want to move, and drag it to its desired location. Figure 18.3
shows a scene being moved down in the playing order.

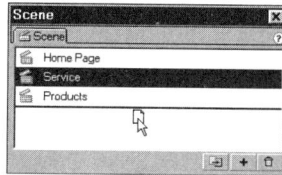

FIGURE 18.3
*You can change the order of scenes in the Scene Panel. In this example, the ser-
vice scene is being moved after the Product scene.*

TIP

> Downloading scenes from a server can disrupt the flow
> of a movie, depending on circumstances beyond the
> control of the Flash designer. It is a good idea to break
> your movie into scenes when the movie is large and
> doing so helps you keep it in manageable segments.

Animated Symbols

Animated symbols are also a method to manage movies that may
grow to contain thousands of layers and hundreds of frames.

Animated symbols are like ordinary symbols except that they have
action. Thus, they can generate motion in your movie while only being
placed in one frame of your Timeline. But they keep on playing—
moving—throughout the entire movie.

Animated symbols can be made from scratch or converted from existing animations.

To create a new symbol:

1. Choose **Insert, New Symbol** from the menu.

2. Choose the **Graphic** button, enter a name, and click **OK**.

3. Create your animated symbol the same way you would create a movie. Select the Timeline frames in which you want the animated symbol to appear. When it is complete, click the Scene link above the Timeline. The symbol will be saved in your movie library.

4. Click the Scene link in the Timeline to return to the movie window. To see the new Symbol, choose **Window**, **Library** to look at the Library Panel. Figure 18.4 shows an animated symbol open in the Library Panel.

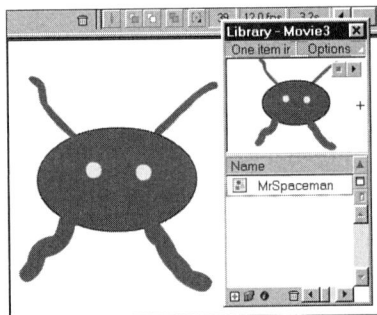

FIGURE 18.4
Animated symbols appear in the Library Panel, and can be recognized by the small play buttons that appear in their upper-right corner.

To convert either a section of a movie or an entire movie into an animated Symbol, first select the frames and layers of the movie you want to convert. Then, choose **Edit**, **Copy Frames** from the menu. This places the selected frames in the Clipboard.

Choose **Insert**, **New Symbol**, choose the **Graphic** option, enter a name for your symbol, and click **OK**. Select the frame in which you want to embed your symbol, and select **Edit**, **Paste Frames**, as shown in Figure 18.5.

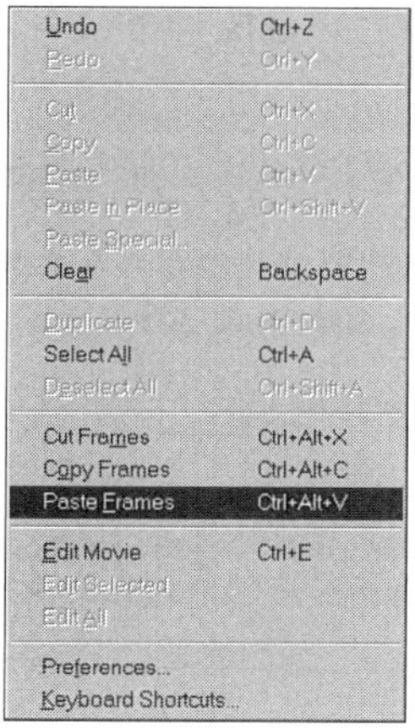

FIGURE 18.5
Existing movies or movie clips can be converted to animated symbols.

Shape tweens are particularly effective as animated tweens. Various rotating, flashing, twinkling, and otherwise active tweens can be converted to and saved as animated graphics symbols, and then placed in movies.

CAUTION

> Animated Symbols appear to be embedded in one frame, but they actually play through many frames. Be careful to have enough frames in your movie when inserting Animated Symbols into it. Have at least as many frames in the movie or layer as there are in the Symbol. For instance, if the animated Symbol has 10 frames, the layer or movie into which it is being inserted must have at least 10 frames.

Movie Clips

Movie Clips are essentially special types of Symbols. They can be inserted anywhere into the movie, and act independently of the movie.

Movie clips are created in a similar fashion to graphic symbols. To create a new movie clip:

1. Choose **Insert**, **New Symbol** from the menu.

2. In the **Symbol Properties** box, choose **Movie Clip**, enter a name for your clip, and select **OK**.

3. Create your clip, making sure to use multiple frames, because this is animation.

4. When the clip is complete, select **Edit**, **Movie** to return to the movie-editing mode.

5. To insert the clip into the movie, choose **Insert**, **Layer** to create a new layer for the clip. Then, with the Library window open, click and drag the clip from the movie library onto the new layer stage.

6. To view the clip, select **Control**, **Test Movie**.

 **TIP**

> Movie clips are best for sequences that you want to play repeatedly throughout your movie. Animated graphics Symbols work best for animation you want to display once.

LESSON 19
Adding Sound

In this lesson, you will learn how to add sound to your movie, how to utilize the Sounds Library, and how to edit and synchronize sounds.

THE SOUNDS LIBRARY

Well-placed and appropriate sound can greatly enhance a Flash movie. Sounds can play through an entire movie, or be associated with particular actions, such as clicking a button. Together with Flash's outstanding animation capacities, voices, music, and other sound can contribute greatly to a true multimedia experience.

The Flash Sounds Library comes with dozens of sounds, such as switches, lights turning off, bricks dropping, and camera shutters clicking. To open the Sounds Library, choose **Window, Common Library, Sounds**.

Most of the sounds found in the Library work best with buttons. With the **Sounds Panel** open, you can test the sounds you want to add to your movie. Click a selection to highlight, and then click the Play arrow in the upper-right corner of the panel window to hear a sample of the sound. Figure 19.1 shows the Sounds Panel extended, and a sound about to be sampled.

FIGURE 19.1
Exploring the Sounds Library. In this example, the sound Switch Camera On is about to be tested.

To add a Library Sound to your movie,

1. Select the frame in which you want the sound to appear, and choose **Insert**, **Keyframe**.

2. Choose **Window**, **Common Libraries**, **Sounds**, and click the name of the sound you want in your movie.

3. Click either the name or the waveform and drag it on to the Stage.

4. Press **Enter** to test your movie and its sound.

TIP

> The waveform that appears in the panel window gives you a basic idea of the length and volume range of the sound. The higher the wave, the louder the sound.

ADDING SOUND TO BUTTONS

Sound associated with buttons can provide a sort of audio indication of the button mode. For instance, a clicking noise associated with the Down State of a button will indicate that it has been pressed.

To add sound to a button symbol, first click the button name in the **Library** window of your movie, or choose a button from the Common Library.

You add sound to the button's Timeline. With a button selected on stage, right-click (Ctrl+click for Macintosh) to get the button pop-up menu. Figure 19.2 shows a button on stage with its menu open.

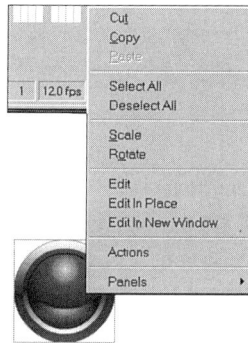

FIGURE 19.2
Sound can be added to a button through the Button pop-up menu.

When you choose **Edit**, the name of the button will appear above your Timeline, just to the right of the Scene number, and a Timeline with the four button modes will appear. Most often, designers will want a sound associated with the Down, and possibly the Over button states.

After deciding what sound you want associated with what button state, click the desired sound in the Sound Library, drag it onto your button on stage, and release. To test the sound, just press **Enter**.

Figure 19.3 shows a button being edited with sound for the **Up**, **Over**, and **Down** states.

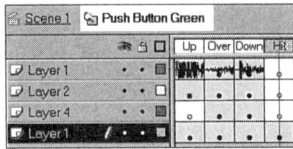

FIGURE 19.3
When sound is added to a button state, a miniature waveform will appear in the frame to which it has been added. In this figure, different sounds have been added to the first three frames.

IMPORTING SOUND

Flash can use sound in many formats, such as MP3, WAV, and AIFF. To import a sound on your hard drive and place it in a movie, first choose **File, Import**. In the dialog box, choose the format you are looking for, and navigate to the folder containing the sound file. Figure 19.4 shows a sound file in WAV format being imported from Windows.

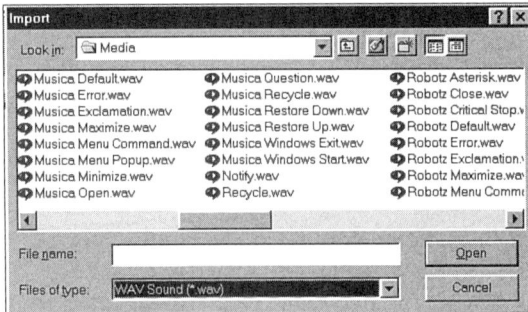

FIGURE 19.4
Sound files from your hard drive can be imported into Flash movies.

Make your selection by clicking the sound file you want to import to highlight it, and then clicking **Open** in the **Import** window. The selected sound file will now appear in your Library, and can be utilized the same way as other sound files.

CAUTION

> There are complex legal issues still being disputed about the use of sound files obtained or exchanged over the Internet. If you have questions about the legality of using an imported sound file, you should make sure you have permission, or consult an authority on these matters.

ADDING SOUND TO FRAMES

Sound files for movies are placed in Keyframes. But although they begin in Keyframes, how long they play is determined by the size of the sound file, and how quickly it downloads in a visitor's browser. This can make precise synchronization of longer sound files with visual frames somewhat tricky. Especially when beginning to use sound with Flash, it is best to develop sound that doesn't require precise coordination with the movie itself.

TIP

> It is definitely recommended that you create a separate layer for sound. In fact, a layer for each sound you add to your movie is a good idea. It is also helpful to name such layers clearly, so you know they are sound layers. This makes it much easier to edit as you make your movie.

To place sound in a Frame, first select the Sound Layer you have created. Open the Library containing your sound, and then click and drag the desired sound onto the Stage. The waveform shape of the sound file will then appear in the Timeline of the sound Layer, beginning in the Keyframe you have selected. Figure 19.5 shows a Layer with sounds beginning in two Keyframes.

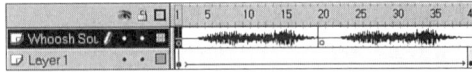

FIGURE 19.5
Waveforms of sound files appear in the Timeline when you add sound to a movie. In this figure, one sound file begins in Frame 1 and another in Frame 19.

You can repeat, or loop, sound files so that they play more than once in your movie.

To loop a sound file:

1. In the sound Layer of your movie, select the Frame in which you want the sound to begin.

2. Open the **Sound** panel by choosing **Window**, **Panels**, **Sound**. Figure 19.6 shows the **Sound Panel**.

3. Enter a value in the Loops box. The sound will repeat that number of times.

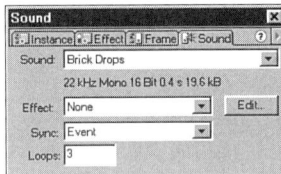

FIGURE 19.6
The Sounds Panel can be used to loop sound files. In this figure, the sound will be repeated three times.

Unless they are stopped, sounds will play until they run through their waveform. To stop a particular sound, first insert a blank Keyframe where you want the sound to stop. Then, open the **Sound Panel** the same way as described previously. Open the drop-down menu for Sound, and choose **None** from the list. To restart a sound in the movie, again insert a Keyframe where you want it to begin, open the **Sound Panel**, and go to the sound drop-down list. This time, select the sound you want to use, then open the **Sync** drop-down menu, and choose **Start**.

LESSON 20
Handling Download Differences; Loading Movies

In this lesson, you will learn how to test your movie in different download speeds, and how to load and launch one movie from within another.

TESTING DOWNLOAD PERFORMANCE

Earlier in this book, I mentioned the importance of keeping your audience in mind when designing Flash movies. Differences in browsers and Internet connections can have a big effect on how a movie downloads, appears, and plays. Many people still use 28.8K modems, for instance, and if your movie is loaded with large audio and bitmap files, it can take some time for it to download in their browsers.

Flash provides the ability to test movies or scenes at different rates, to see how they look and sound.

Test a scene by selecting **Control**, **Test Scene**, or test the entire movie by selecting **Control**, **Test Movie** from the toolbar. In both cases, your movie will open in the Flash player.

In the Flash Player, click the **Debug** menu. A panel with options for connection speeds will drop down. Select one in which you want to test your movie. Figure 20.1 shows the **Debug** selection being made.

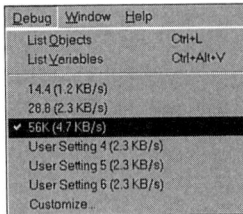

FIGURE 20.1
This movie is being tested to see how it would look using a 56K modem.

TIP

You can test at higher bit rates by clicking the **Customize** option, and entering in numeric values of your own choosing.

The **Bandwidth Profiler** is a Flash feature that enables you to see where potential download problems may occur in your movie. Activate this feature by selecting **View**, **Bandwidth Profiler**. Figure 20.2 shows the **Bandwidth Profiler** activated.

A red horizontal line in the **Bandwidth Profiler** indicates the points at which the movie will have to pause, even if briefly, to download information. If a vertical bar extends above the red line, the movie will pause there when playing.

The **Streaming** view of the **Bandwidth Profiler** displays a bar that indicates the proportion of the file downloaded to the displaying computer. To select this option, choose **View**, **Show Streaming**.

TIP

It's a good idea to test your movie frequently with the **Bandwidth Profiler** as you develop it. This helps identify and rectify potential playback problems while the whole moviemaking process is still underway rather than after you think you have completed it.

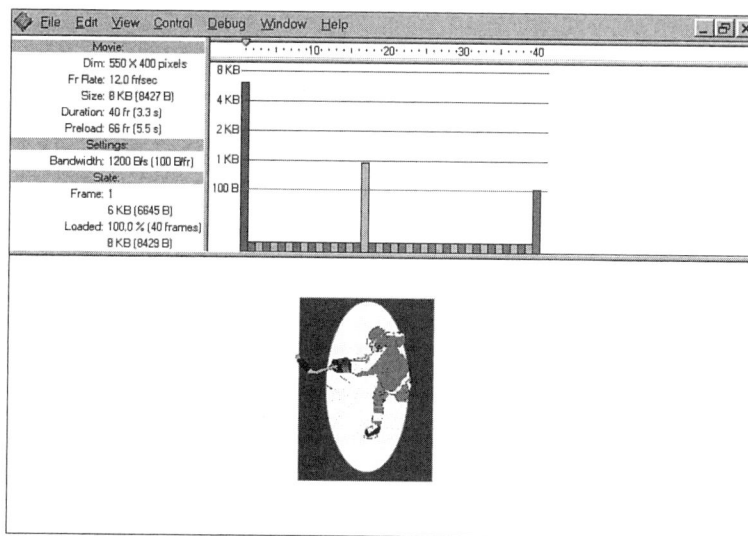

FIGURE 20.2
The Bandwidth Profiler provides detailed information about how your movie will download.

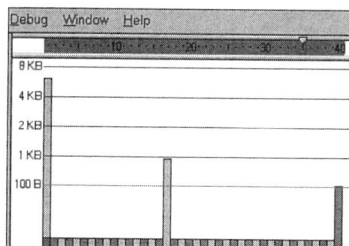

FIGURE 20.3
*In **Show Streaming** view, the green bar across the Timeline indicates the amount of the file that is downloaded.*

You can compensate for uneven download time by looping, or repeating, a portion of your movie until all the movie components are downloaded and ready to play. Visitors seeing your movie on browsers with fast Web connections may not need the added time, but large bitmap and audio files may take longer for some computers. This technique enables you to mesh the sound and visual effects for everyone.

1. First, determine in what frame the download slowdown occurs.

2. Select a frame at which you want all the action and sound to mesh, usually right after the one in which there is a slow-down. Choose **Insert**, **Blank Keyframe**.

3. Select the frame, and then choose **Window**, **Actions**.

4. Click the Plus sign, and choose **Actions**, **ifFrameLoaded**. Figure 20.4 shows this selection being made.

5. Enter the frame at which the download snag occurs.

6. With the **ifFrameLoaded** command still selected, click the Plus icon and choose **Basic Actions**, **Go To**. Enter the frame to which the movie will jump when all the elements in the frame defined in step 5 are loaded.

7. Finally, you must decide what to do if the frame specified in step 5 is not loaded. To do so, create a new blank Keyframe after the Keyframe defined in step 5. Select the new Keyframe, click the Plus icon, and choose **Basic Actions**, **Go To**. The default settings will send the movie back to frame 1, or you can enter a new frame value if you choose.

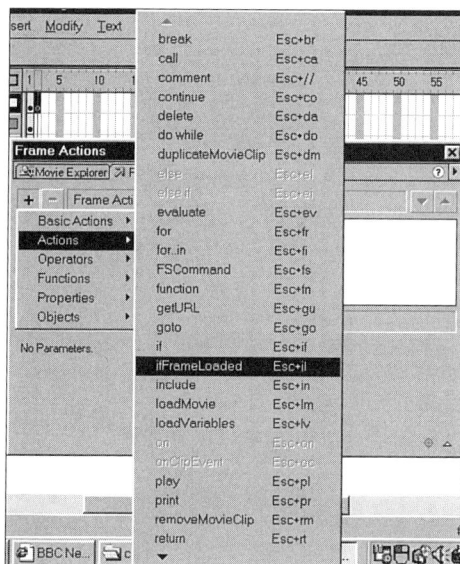

FIGURE 20.4
You can loop your movie until frames with large downloads are fully loaded and ready to play.

LOADING AND LAUNCHING MOVIES

Flash can be programmed to launch, or start, one movie from within another. Also, movies can be superimposed, or placed one on top of another. These techniques can be valuable in making large movies more manageable and faster, and in enabling you to develop an entire Web site in Flash.

To load a movie into another movie, first create the movie that will contain the common components of all the movies. This would mean, for example, the navigation buttons, and perhaps things such as a company logo, or family crest and motto.

NEW TERM

A **container** movie is the movie into which other movies are loaded.

Select the frame in which you want your superimposed, or loaded, movie, to launch. Choose **Window**, **Actions** to get the **Frame Actions Panel.** Click the Plus icon, **Basic Actions**, **Load Movie**, as shown in Figure 20.5.

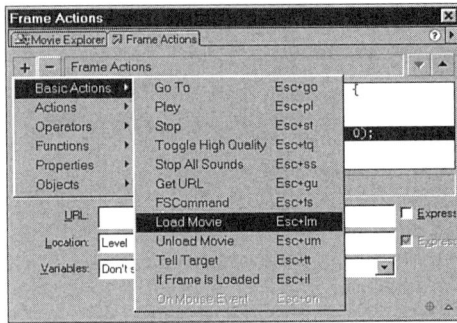

FIGURE 20.5
One movie can be loaded—superimposed or inserted—into another.

In the URL box of the **Frame Actions** panel, enter the *Flash*.swf* name of the movie that will load. You can layer the movies by selecting **Level** from the drop-down list and entering **1** in the box. The new movie will be loaded one level, or layer, above the container movie. You can specify different levels as you create new movies to load into the original container movie. The higher the number of a movie in a series of levels, the closer it appears to the top.

Test your new movie as you would others, by selecting **Control**, **Test Movie**.

TIP

Loading movies into one another, rather than creating multiple scenes in the same movie, can result in significant reduction of file size, and therefore download time.

Movies can be unloaded from each other. Go to the **Frame Actions** panel as in the preceding steps, again click the Plus sign, and select **Basic Actions**, **Unload Movie**. Select the level movie you want to unload.

LESSON 21

Collecting and Displaying Information

In this lesson, you will learn how to collect information from your site visitors.

STOP ACTION IN A FRAME

In Lesson 15, "Assigning Actions to Buttons," you learned of forms of interactivity that enable viewers to stop and restart the movie, jump to certain points in it, or jump to other Web sites. Other forms of interactivity enable visitors to enter information that customizes the presentation for them. For example, a site visitor may enter information on a model and year of car they are looking for, and the movie can display a segment on that type of car.

To collect data from site visitors, the first thing you need to do is stop the movie. If you want to review actions such as Stop and Play, go back to Lesson 15.

Actions can be associated with Frames, as well as with Buttons. This means that the movie action will occur regardless of any action taken by the site visitor.

To assign stop action to a Frame, first make sure there are no objects selected. Then select **Window**, **Actions** to open the **Frame Actions** panel. Click the Plus icon, and select **Basic Actions**, **Stop**, as shown in Figure 21.1 This will stop your movie in the selected Frame.

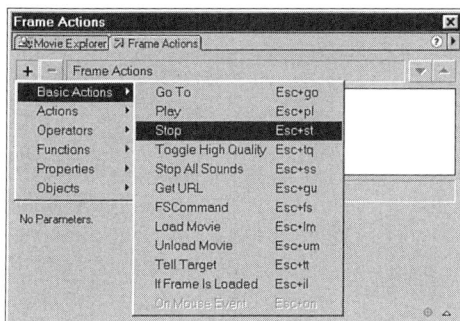

FIGURE 21.1
Actions can be added to frames as well as to Buttons.

CAUTION

> Any layer can have actions. But as a practical matter, it is best to have them assigned to a single layer, usually the top layer. This arrangement makes managing the actions much simpler.

COLLECTING INFORMATION

With the action in your movie stopped, you can collect information or data from your visitors, and display information back to them. Doing this requires two text fields, one to collect data and one to display it, and a button to execute the action that takes data from one text field and displays it in the other.

NEW TERM

> A **text field** is a text box with the ability to collect and/or display information.

Create a text field by drawing an ordinary text box using the **Text** tool. Then select the text box and choose **Text**, **Options** from the toolbar. This opens the **Text Options** panel.

Open the **Text-Type** drop-down list by clicking the downward-pointing arrow, and select **Input Text**, as shown in Figure 21.2.

> **TIP**
>
> Flash, by default, enters a name for your text field. To change the name, enter one in the Collecting Information **Variable** field. Again, it is very helpful to come up with a good naming system, particularly because you need to coordinate the information entered into the field with the information returned to the viewer.

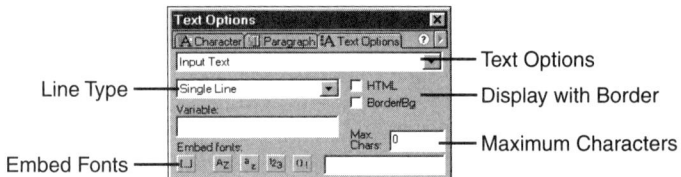

FIGURE 21.2
Fields to collect data from visitors can be created in the Text Options panel.

- The **Line Type** entry lets you choose a single line of input for such things as names and addresses, or multiline input for information requiring more than one line. The Password option in this box will display as asterisks.

- The **HTML** check box changes the input to Hypertext Markup Language, the computer language of Web sites, when the movie is published.

- The **Border/BG** box places a border around the input field.

- The **Max.Chars** (Maximum Characters) box restricts the number of characters (numbers and letters) entered in the field.

- The **Embed Fonts** icon determines how the text displays when it is entered in a field.

Next, you will need a field to display the collected data. Again, create the text box with the **Text** tool and open the **Text Options** panel.

> ### CAUTION
>
> Even though you are creating a text field to *display* collected information, you still select the **Input Text** option in the **Text Options** panel.

Enter a name in the variable for your text field. Figure 21.3 shows a text field with a new name entered.

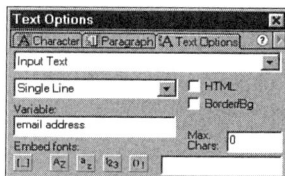

FIGURE 21.3
Entering names (variables) that correspond to the information you are collecting will make it a lot easier to keep track of your various text boxes.

The third step in collecting data capabilities is creating a button that moves visitors from the input field to the output field.

> ### TIP
>
> You will need the *exact* names of your input and output text fields. You should write them down.

To create a button that will initiate the desired action, place (or create) a button on your Stage, and select it. Then open the **Object Actions** panel by selecting **Window, Actions**. Choose **Basic Actions, On Mouse Event** from the Plus sign flyout menu. With this line still selected, click the Plus icon again, and choose **Actions, Set Variable** from the flyout menu. You may have to toggle down the menu to see this selection, shown in Figure 21.4.

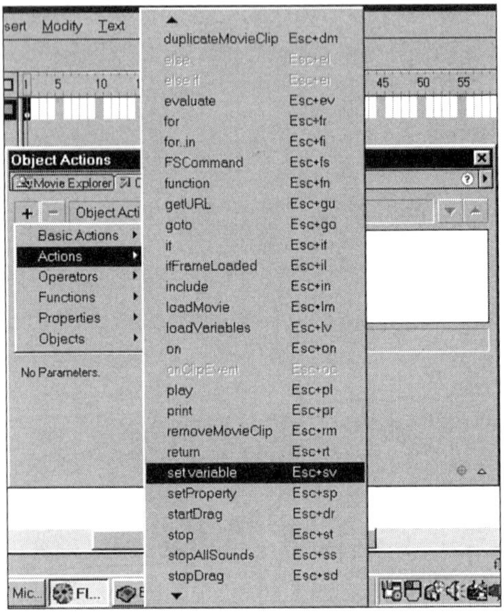

FIGURE 21.4
Creating a button that triggers information collection.

In the **Variable** box, enter the name of the text box that will display
the collected data. In the **Value** box, enter the name assigned to the
box that collects the data, and check the lower **Expression** box. When
you have finished, you will have generated Action Script, and the
Object Actions panel should resemble the one shown in Figure 21.5.

NEW TERM

> The names can get confusing, but try to remember that
> **Value** is the name of the text field that *collects* data;
> **Variable** is the name of the text field that *displays* data.

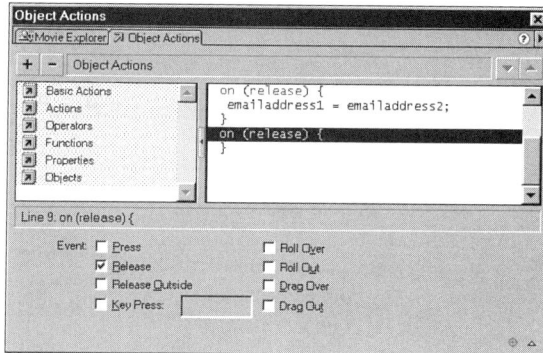

FIGURE 21.5
Use the Object Actions panel to determine what mouse action will initiate inter-activity.

CALCULATING DATA

You can perform calculations, such as determining the amount taken off the price of a discounted item, with Flash interactivity.

First, create and name two text fields as in the previous example, one to collect and one to display data, and place a button on the Stage. With the button selected, choose **Window**, **Actions** to again open the **Object Actions** panel. Click the Plus icon, and select **Basic Actions**, **On Mouse Event**.

With On Mouse Event still highlighted, click the Plus icon again, and select **Actions**, **Set Variables**. In the **Variable** box, enter the name of the text field that will display the data. Don't check the **Expression** box. Type in the name of the text field that will be used to collect data in the **Value** box. This time, check the **Expression** box.

Then, put in a calculation expression. The example in Figure 21.6 shows minus 5.

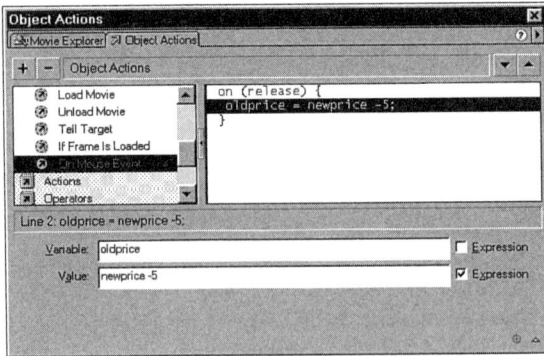

FIGURE 21.6
Numbers entered in the Value field will have 5 subtracted from them, and be displayed in the Variable field.

TIP

Calculation expressions are + to add, - to subtract, / to divide, and * to multiply.

Lesson 22
Importing to Flash

In this lesson, you will learn how to import drawings and other objects from other programs into Flash, and incorporate them into your movie. You will also learn how to convert bitmap images into vector images.

Importing Bitmap Images

Flash does well at drawing and designing, but it is not mainly a drawing program. As you develop your ability to make movies with Flash, you will most likely want to incorporate images created in other programs, including bitmap image. This process is called *importing*.

In Lesson 1, "Meet Flash 5," you learned that Flash works primarily with vector images, not bitmapped images. But many images, including some you may want to utilize, are done in bitmap format. Bitmap images are in such formats such as GIF, JPEG, PNG, PSG, and EPS.

Flash allows you to import bitmap images and incorporate them in your movie, or to convert them to vector images. As mentioned earlier, bitmap images take up a lot more space than vector graphics. But sometimes using a bitmap is necessary or useful for your movie.

NEW TERM

A **bitmap image** is made of numerous dots called pixels. Each location and description (color) of the pixel is stored in the bitmap, so the image is defined as a series of pixels, rather than lines and curves, as in vector images. The same basic image done as a bitmap or a vector will thus have a considerably larger file size as a bitmap.

Import a bitmap file by choosing **File**, **Import**. In the **Import** dialog box, make sure **All Formats** is selected, as shown in Figure 22.1. This will ensure that all importable graphic files are displayed.

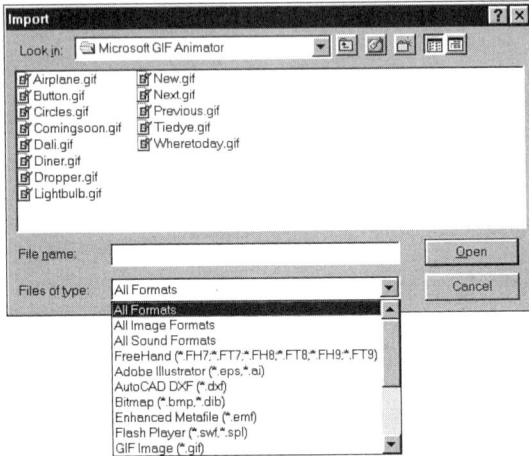

FIGURE 22.1
Files in many formats can be imported to Flash.

Make sure that the Frame of your Timeline into which you want to insert the bitmap is selected. Then, double-click the file you want to import.

You can also import bitmaps using the **Copy** and **Paste** commands. Create or open a bitmap, and then choose **Edit**, **Copy** to place it in the Clipboard. Then, open your Flash movie, select the Frame into which you want the bitmap to be imported, and select **Edit**, **Paste**.

Bitmap images can be manipulated by scaling, rotating, skewing, and moving, similar to Flash Drawings.

You can also break apart a bitmap, and modify selected portions of it, including reproducing part of it.

1. First, choose **File**, **Import**.

2. Navigate to the folder containing the desired bitmap image and select **Open** to import the image.

3. Select the bitmap with the **Arrow** tool, and choose **Modify**, **Break Apart**, as shown in Figure 22.2. The appearance of the image will appear faded.

4. Select the **Oval** or **Rectangle** tool to draw a shape on stage. The image from the bitmap will appear in the shape. You can then select the image with the **Arrow** tool and manipulate it to a desired shape; the bitmap will expand or contract to fill the shape. Figure 22.3 shows two bitmaps, one that was broken apart and used to fill an oval that was then altered slightly.

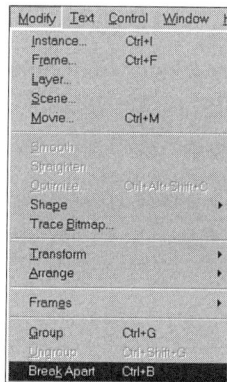

FIGURE 22.2

The Break Apart selection can allow you to select a portion of an imported image you want to reproduce.

FIGURE 22.3
Bitmaps can be used to fill shapes, which can then be further manipulated.

You can also use the **Lasso** and **Magic Wand** tools to change the colors of selected portions of bitmap images. Again, bring the bitmap onto the Stage by using the previously described steps. Choose **Modify**, **Break Apart**, and then click outside the image to deselect it.

Next, click the **Magic Wand** button in the toolbox. Open the **Magic Wand Settings** box by clicking the **Magic Wand Properties** button. Figure 22.4 shows the **Magic Wand Settings** dialog box.

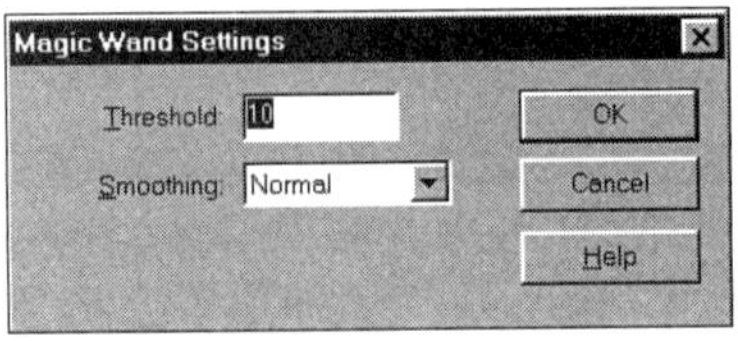

FIGURE 22.4
The Magic Wand Settings box. Threshold settings go from 1 to 200. A lower Threshold setting means that Flash is less likely to select similar colors.

Click the bitmap with the **Magic Wand** tool to select the color you want to alter. The selected areas will appear permeated with white dots. Click the **Fill** color palette, and browse and click to select the color you want to fill the selected area. Click outside the image to end the process.

You can then move, edit, or delete this new image as you would any other selected image. Figure 22.5 shows two images, one that has been created by breaking apart a bitmap and changing its coloration.

FIGURE 22.5
Bitmap images can be broken apart and manipulated with the Magic Wand tool.

CONVERTING BITMAPS TO VECTORS

Bitmap images can be converted to vectors, thus allowing you the same ability to work with them and modify them as you would any other vector in Flash.

CAUTION

Converting an image from bitmap to vector does not really cut down on file size. In some cases, it may actually increase it. Images that have a lot of solid color areas and line art are generally most suited for conversion from bitmap to vector.

Follow these steps to convert a bitmap to a vector.

1. Choose **File, Import** and navigate to the bitmap destined for conversion, and click **Open** to import it to your movie.

2. Choose **Modify, Trace Bitmap**. The **Trace Bitmap** dialog box, shown in Figure 22.6, appears.

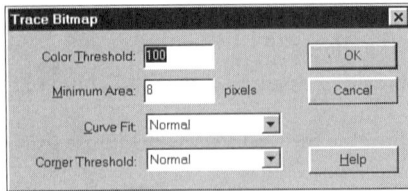

FIGURE 22.6
The Trace Bitmap dialog box enables you to adjust the settings for converted bitmaps.

3. Enter a value between 1 and 500 in the **Color Threshold** field. A larger number contains fewer colors than the original, reducing file size, but also image quality.

4. In the **Minimum Area** field, enter a number between 1 and 1,000. Again, higher numbers reduce file size but also quality.

5. Select a choice from the **Curve Fit** drop-down menu. Tighter curves more closely match curves and shapes in the original, and have a larger file size.

6. From the **Corner Threshold** drop-down menu, choose a selection. **Many Corners** maintains sharper edges, whereas **Few Corners** smoothes out some edges.

7. Click **OK** when you have finished.

Experiment when converting bitmaps to vectors, to achieve the best effects for your purpose. Tracing can take time and patience, and you will definitely learn how to develop what effects you want as you gain experience.

LESSON 23
Going Online

In this lesson, you will learn how to prepare and optimize your movies for viewing on the Internet.

EXPORTING TO THE FLASH PLAYER

Movies made with Flash are viewed through the Flash player, which is available free at www.macromedia.com.

The first step in making a movie ready for viewing in the Flash Player is to make certain it is saved as an *.swf file. This can be done either by exporting or publishing the movie.

> **TIP**
>
> Flash movies have the file extension ***fla**. This means that they can be opened only in Flash. When that movie becomes an *.swf file, it can then be viewed by people with the Flash Player.

To export a movie to the Flash Player, first open the file, and then choose **File**, **Export Movie**. Choose **Flash Player (*.swf)** from the **Save As Type** drop-down menu as shown in Figure 23.1. Navigate to the folder in which you want to save the movie, and click **OK**.

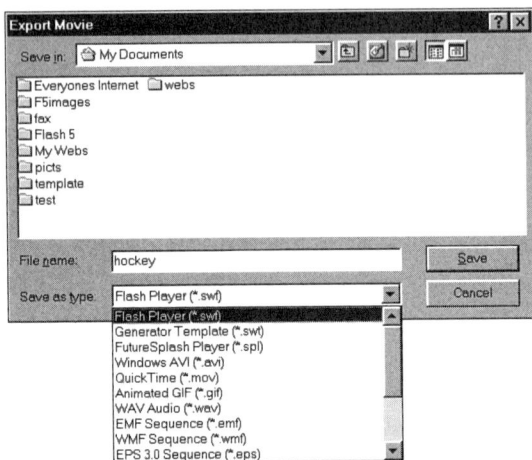

FIGURE 23.1
Flash Movies must be saved in the *.swf format to be viewed in the Flash Player.

CAUTION

You can also save by choosing **File**, **Publish** from the tool-bar. But this method uses the same folder and filename you already are using; it doesn't allow you to select a folder and change the filename.

When you open and test your movie, you can zoom in or out by selecting **View**, **Zoom In**, or **Zoom Out**. This can be helpful in providing another angle on your movie. When you select **Zoom In**, the cursor becomes a hand that allows you to grab and move different parts of the screen. You can also **Rewind**, **Stop**, and **Loop** the movie while testing.

SYNCHRONIZING YOUR SOUND

Before you make your movie available on the Internet, there are likely to be some last stage checks you will want to make.

If the sound is not synchronized exactly the way you want it to be, you can make adjustments in the **Sound Panel**. To edit a sound, first click the sound in the Timeline, or select it in the current Library. Then, go to **Window**, **Panels**, **Sound**, and open the **Sync** drop-down menu, as shown in Figure 23.2.

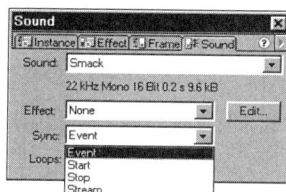

FIGURE 23.2
The Sound Panel enables you to synchronize your audio and visual effects exactly as you like.

The **Event** option in this menu starts the sound at the same time as a visual event. For instance, if a car appears in your movie in Keyframe 10, you can add the sound of an engine starting in Keyframe 10, and use this option to ensure that the start of the sound is in sync with the appearance of the car.

The **Start** option is similar, except that it ensures that the second instance of a sound will not begin until the first is completed. For example, if another car appears in Frame 35 of the movie, the sound should be set to **Start** sync. This will prevent overlapping of a sound used more than once.

The **Stop** option ends a sound at a specific Keyframe. To use this option, go to the Timeline frame in which you want the sound to stop, and choose **Insert**, **Keyframe**. Choose the sound you want to stop, and select **Stop** in the **Sync** drop-down menu.

The **Stream** sync option compels the animation to maintain pace with the sound, even if it must drop frames to do so. **Stream** is also the only sync option that stops playing when the movie stops.

CAUTION

The **Stream** option can be very useful when Flash movies are put on the Internet. But visual quality of the movie can suffer if Flash is forced to drop frames to keep up with the sound. Be sure to test the movie thoroughly if you use this option.

You can also stop all sounds at a specific frame in the movie. To stop all sounds, first choose **Insert Layer**, and place the new layer on top of the Timeline. Click in the Timeline where you want the sounds to stop, and select **Insert**, **Keyframe**. Then, select this Keyframe, and open the **Frame Actions** panel by choosing **Window**, **Actions**.

Click the Plus icon, and go to **Basic Actions**, **Stop All Sounds**, as shown in Figure 23.3.

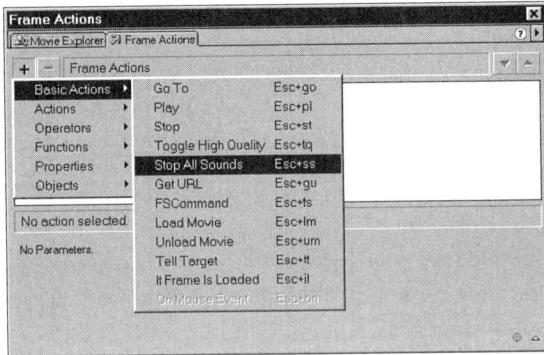

FIGURE 23.3
All sound in your movie comes to a halt with this option.

Fine-Tuning Your Movie

TIP

By now you've probably come to realize that just about every decision you make in Flash involves balancing appearance and impact with size. It can be a struggle to keep your movie at a manageable size, and to optimize the movie's impact you have to continually evaluate your options in the context of what you are trying to achieve overall with your movie. Such is life on the Web.

Review many elements of your movie before final publication. Oftentimes, you will be surprised at the amount of file space reduction you can achieve.

Flash takes some steps to optimize your movie as you are publishing it. For instance, it compacts nested groups (multiple groups linked to one another) into one group. It also will automatically put duplicate shapes into the file only one time. But, there are other final editing measures you can take that also reduce size and maximize your movie's impact.

- Gradient fills can look fine, but they take up a lot of space. Use them judiciously.

- Imported sound is best in the MP3 format. Not only is this format highly compressed, thus taking up less space than the WAV format, but the sound quality is higher. Figure 23.4 shows a sound being selected in MP3 format.

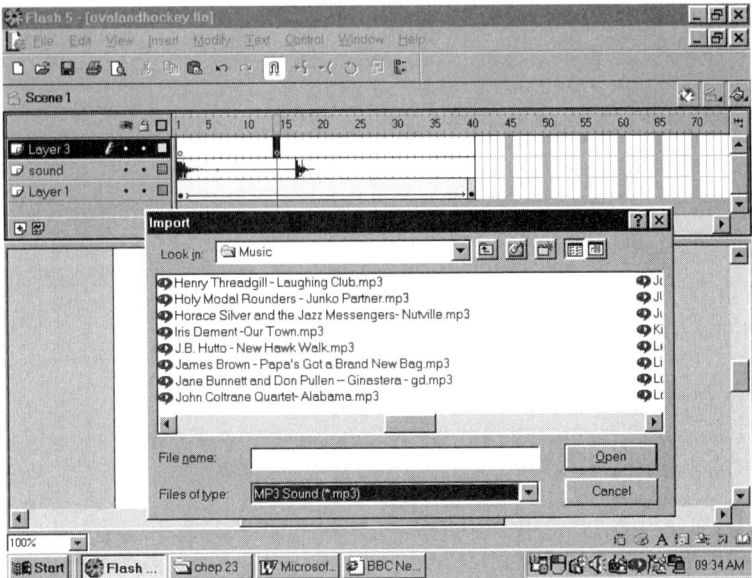

FIGURE 23.4
MP3 sound files provide better-quality sound and take up less space.

- Keeping your font size, color, and style consistent can also contribute to file size reduction.

- Making sure you used tweened animation, rather than frame by frame animation, is important. The multiple Keyframes needed in frame by frame animation can bulk up the file size in a hurry.

- You can also find ways to reduce file size by optimizing curved shapes, specifically those imported from other programs. Quite frequently, what appears to be one curve actually contains multiple segments, each of which is a Flash object. Reducing the number of segments in a curve reduces file size.

To optimize curve shapes, first select the object you want to optimize. Choose **Modify**, **Optimize** from the toolbar. The **Optimize Curves** dialog box, shown in Figure 23.5, will appear.

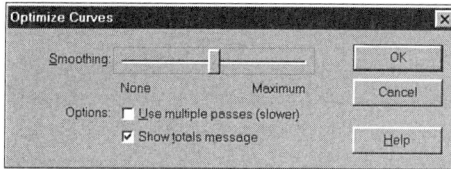

FIGURE 23.5
Optimizing your curves can help reduce file size and facilitate the downloading and playing of your movie.

Click the **Smoothing** slider, and drag to a desired point in the range from **None** to **Maximum**. The closer to the **Maximum** point you set it, the smoother the curves and the smaller the file sizes will be.

The **Use Multiple Passes** option will be slower, but it will also result in the maximum optimization of your selected curve. You can see the results of your curve optimization by clicking in the **Show Totals Message** check box. Click **OK** to accept the curve and end the optimization process.

LESSON 24
Putting Flash on the Web

In this lesson, you learn how to add a Flash movie to a Web site.

FLASH AND HTML

HyperText Markup Language (HTML) is the universal language of the Web. It is a form of code that enables Web browsers, the two most popular of which are Internet Explorer and Netscape, to interpret and display graphics, text, and even Flash movies.

Flash can generate HTML for you, even if you don't know any, and embed a Flash movie in it. In other words, the HTML page acts as a sort of container for the Flash movie.

TIP

You can design an all-Flash Web site. The main drawback of this approach is that you won't be able to combine easily edited HTML with the Flash movie. Many programs enable you to generate your own HTML Web pages without knowing HTML, but it is worth your while to learn some as you begin designing Web pages. A knowledge of even a small number of basic HTML commands can provide a platform for learning more, and will enable you to gain more direct control over the appearance and content of your site.

SELECTING YOUR SETTINGS

Open the **Publish Settings** dialog box, shown in Figure 24.1, by
selecting **File, Publish Settings**.

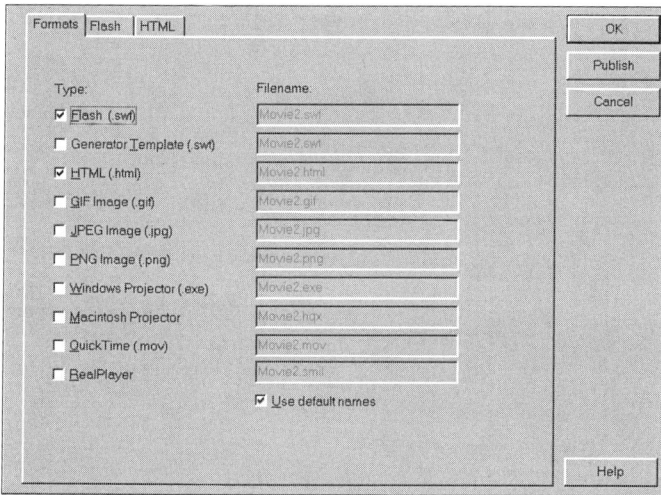

FIGURE 24.1
*The **Publish Settings** dialog box. The **Flash (*.swf)** and **HTML (.html)** options are
checked by default.*

NEW TERM

SWF stands for Shock Wave File. Shock Wave is another
name Macromedia has used for the Flash Player. Flash
Player files have the *.swf extension.

With both of the default options checked, you automatically generate
an HTML page with a movie embedded in it. The File and folder
names you originally assigned in your Flash file are assigned again,
unless you deselect the **Use Default Names** check box.

Click the **HTML** tag in the **Publish Settings** box to bring forward the panel where you make HTML choices for the Web page accompanying your movie. Figure 24.2 shows the **Publish Settings** dialog box with the **HTML** tab clicked.

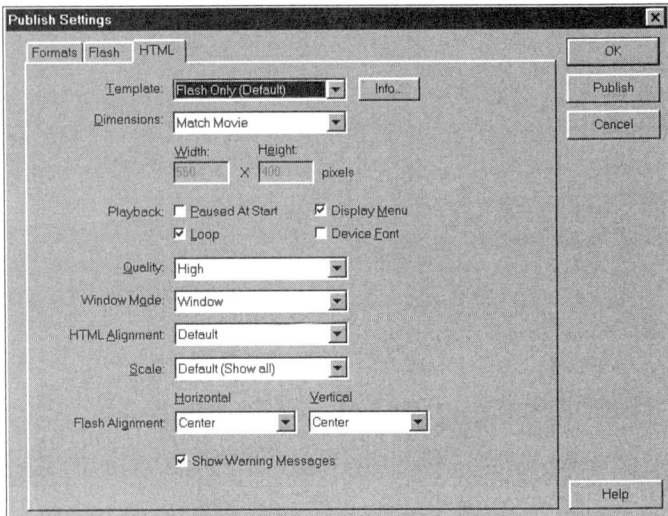

FIGURE 24.2
It is often best and easiest to accept the default HTML values Flash offers.

If you accept the default values, you can still edit that page with your own HTML code, or with a Web page editor.

There are numerous options in this panel.

- In the **Template** drop-down menu, choose **Flash Only** or one of the other options. Usually, **Flash Only** will make your movie accessible in most browsers. Click the **Info** button to get information about each selection. Figure 24.3 shows the **Info** button clicked with the **Flash Only** selection made.

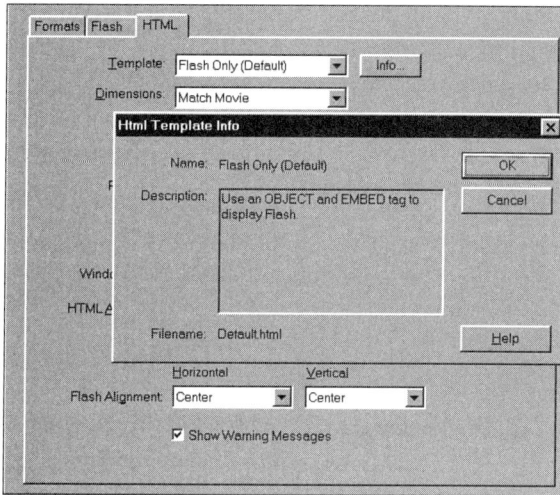

FIGURE 24.3
Flash displays information on publishing options.

- Choose a movie size in the **Dimensions** drop-down menu. **Match Movie** means that the Flash movie will display at the same size as your movie project. To size a movie differently, select either **Pixels** or **Percent**, and enter the desired dimensions.

- The **Playback** options control user interaction with the movie. **Paused at Start** requires a viewer click to start the movie, either on a button or by selecting **Play**. **Loop** repeats the movie continuously. Deselect this if you don't want that effect. **Display Menu** shows a context menu when the visitor right-clicks in Windows or Command+clicks in Mac. **Device Font** works only with Windows, and allows you to substitute for fonts that don't reside on the visitor's system. Be careful, because this option can change the appearance of your movie from the original design.

- The **Quality** drop-down menu enables you to determine whether to emphasize quick playback speed or high image quality when your movie plays. A movie played back at **High** or **Best** will have the highest visual quality, but play at a lower speed. The reverse is true for **Low** or **Auto Low**.

- The **Window Mode** menu utilizes features available only in certain browsers. The default setting, **Window**, displays the Flash movie in its own window; the other settings either place Web page elements behind the movie (**Opaque**) or show the Web page through transparent sections of your movie (**Transparent Windowless**).

- The **HTML Alignment** drop-down menu controls the positioning of the Flash movie window in the browser window. **Default** centers the movie; other options move it up or down, right or left editor.

- Choose **Default** from the **Scale** drop-down menu, unless for some reason you defined a movie display window different from the size of the movie in the Dimensions area.

- Make certain the **Show Warning Messages** box is checked, so that any possible clashes between the HTML selections you made are displayed in Flash, for you the developer.

- Click **Publish**, and then **OK**.

The **Flash** tab in the **Publish Settings** box allows you to configure and adjust the settings for published movies. Click the **Flash** tab to see the panel shown in Figure 24.4.

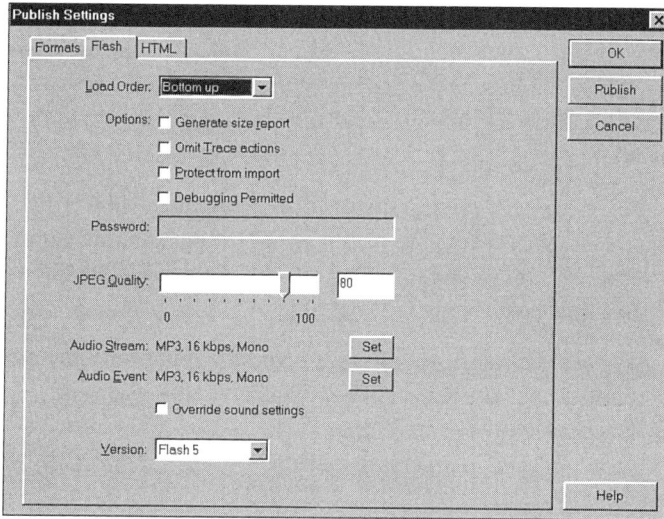

FIGURE 24.4
*The Flash tab in the **Publish Settings** panel enables you to protect your file from being edited by others, to control the layering order of the movie, and to decide the highest version of Flash that will be supported by the movie.*

1. The **Load Order** drop-down menu enables you to select the order in which the Flash Player loads your movie layers. **Bottom up** loads the lowest layers first; **Top down** does the opposite.

2. The **Options** section of the panel has several selections. **Generate Size Report** lists the amount of data in each frame. **Protect from Import** keeps other people from importing your movie into their own Flash movies or projects. **Omit Trace Actions** is an advanced feature that prevents a Flash window from opening and displaying comments; you usually won't need to select it. If other people are going to be working from other computers to help you debug snags in your movies, select the **Debugging Permitted** option. You must enter a password for this and the **Protect from Import** option.

3. The **JPEG Quality** slider button influences movie quality by controlling the compression of your bitmaps. A higher setting means a higher image quality, but, as is often the case in Flash, the trade-off is a larger file size. Again, experimentation is helpful.

4. The **Audio Stream** setting controls audio files whose sync was set to **Stream**. The **Audio Event** setting controls those that were set to **Event** or **Start**. Click **Set** to open the **Sound Settings** box, shown in Figure 24.5.

5. Choose a Flash version from the **Version** drop-down menu. Flash 5 contains features not available in all versions of Flash, but you can make your movie so that it will be completely played in any Flash version.

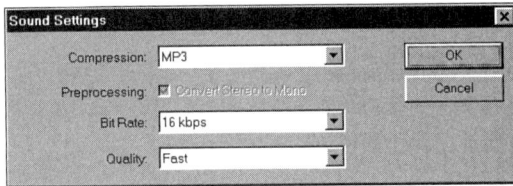

FIGURE 24.5
The **Sound Settings** panel enables you to choose the Compression Type of your movie's sound. If you choose **Disable**, the sound will have the same settings as it does in the movie Library.

TIP

Some visitors who view your movie may not have the latest version of the Flash Player on their computer. You may want to provide a link to Macromedia, where it can be downloaded free and your movie can be viewed in all its up-to-date splendor.

LESSON 25
Exporting Flash

In this lesson, you will learn how to export Flash movies and graphics so that they can be viewed in other formats.

EXPORTING STATIC GRAPHICS

Exporting Flash means taking all or part of your movie and making it available for use in other formats. This can be useful for several reasons, including utilizing images you've created in one movie as graphics in another Web page, and making your movie available to a wider range of viewers.

A single frame of a Flash movie can be saved as a static graphic, and exported for use in other projects. To save and export a static graphic image, first click the Frame in the Timeline you want to save, thus selecting everything on that Frame and Layer. If you want to save a particular image, click it with the **Arrow** tool to select it. Figure 25.1 shows Frame 20 being selected.

Then, choose **File**, **Export Image**. The **Export Image** dialog box, shown in Figure 25.2, appears.

Navigate to the folder on your system where you want to save the file, and enter a name in the **File Name** field. Choose a format from the **Save As Type** drop-down menu.

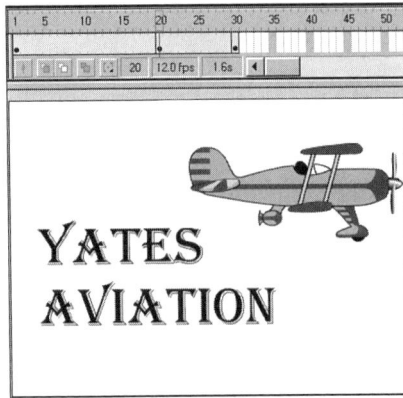

FIGURE 25.1
Selecting Frame 20 for export as a static graphic.

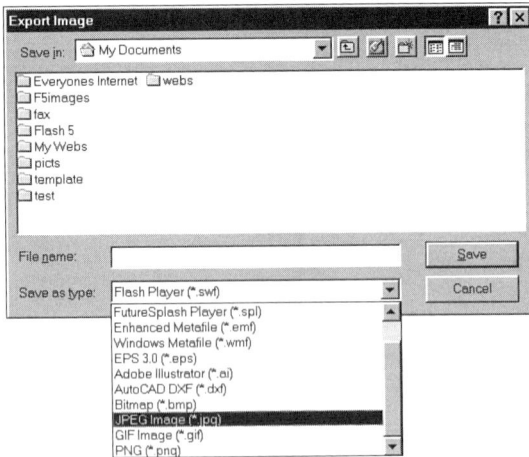

FIGURE 25.2
*Choose a filename, a folder, and a format for your exported image in the **Export
Image** dialog box.*

EXPORT OPTIONS

Flash provides many choices for export formats. But if you want to display a frame of your movie on the Web, your basic and most frequently used options are GIF and JPEG.

JPEG is best for exporting complex images with attributes such as gradient fills, photos, and other images with nuanced color schemes. When you choose JPEG, you will see the dialog box shown in Figure 25.3.

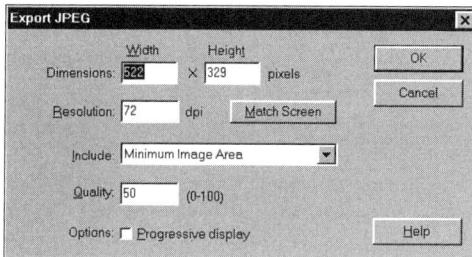

FIGURE 25.3
You can determine the resolution and dimensions of your Frame exported to JPEG.

The **Quality** option in the dialog box has a range from 0 to 100. The higher you go, the higher the quality of the image will be. It will also have a larger file size and take longer to download.

TIP

Quite often when exporting JPEG files, a higher-quality setting will not result in an image with a significantly larger file size, but a low-quality setting can result in a degraded image. Experiment with this feature to achieve the best results for your purpose.

If you select the GIF format when exporting your Frame or object, the **GIF** dialog box appears. Exporting in the GIF format allows for interlacing and transparency. Figure 25.4 shows the **Export GIF** dialog box with interlacing and transparency checked.

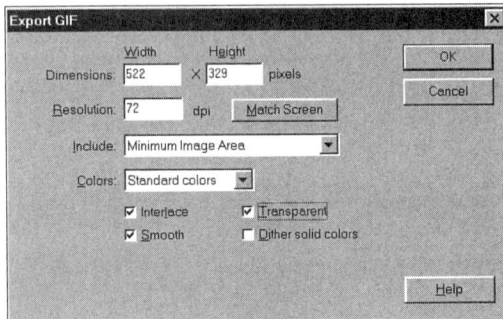

FIGURE 25.4
The Export GIF dialog box.

> **NEW TERM**
>
> **Interlacing** describes a process in which a downloading image resolves in more and more detail throughout the entire image, rather than unfolding from top to bottom. **Transparency** means that the background of an image will not appear when the image is put on the Web.

Exported images can be edited and changed. In other words, exported vectors can be edited in another vector-editing program, and exported bitmaps can be edited in bitmap-editing programs.

EXPORTING MOVIES TO OTHER FORMATS

Entire movies can be exported, for use in other projects, or for viewing in other formats.

Choose **File**, **Export Movie** to open the **Export Movie** dialog box, shown in Figure 25.5.

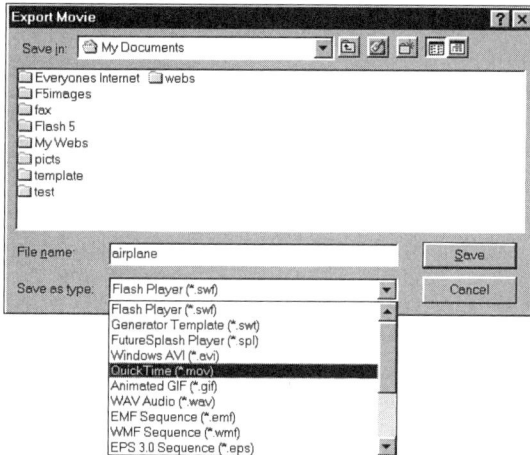

FIGURE 25.5
*The **Export Movie** dialog box.*

In the **Export Movie** dialog box, navigate to the folder in which you are going to save the file, and enter a name for the file in the text field. Choose the file format in which you want to save the movie from the **Save As Type** drop-down list. Click **Save**, and click **OK** to finish the export.

The three main format choices for exported movies are AVI, QuickTime, and Animated GIF. Once again, deciding which way you want to go is largely a matter of weighing the questions of image quality and download speed. Image quality is better in AVI and QuickTime. But the file sizes are larger.

Animated GIFs can be viewed in most versions of Internet Explorer and Netscape Navigator, and only viewers with old browsers will not be able to see them. AVI files can be seen by Windows users, and QuickTIme by Mac users.

If you choose the AVI format, you will see the **Export Windows AVI** dialog box, as shown in Figure 25.6.

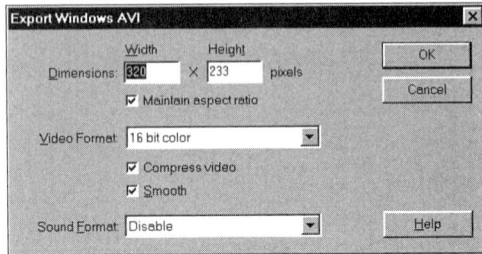

FIGURE 25.6
The dialog box for exporting to AVI format.

The default dimensions in the **Export Windows AVI** dialog box express a size that will capture your entire movie in AVI format. If, for some reason, you decide to change these values, you should check the **Maintain Aspect Ratio** box to make sure the proportions of the movie remain unchanged.

The **Video Format** drop-down menu allows you to select between 8-, 16-, 24-, and 32-bit color. 8-bit color takes less file space, and is almost always enough to maintain the colors of Flash movies.

The **Sound Format** drop-down menu provides choices for the movie's sound quality. Flash suggests a sound format based on your sound files, and will suggest Disable if you have no sound. If you decide to select your own choice, you can decrease the file size by selecting a lower Mhz or bit value.

After you have made your selections and clicked **OK**, the **Video Compression** dialog box opens (see Figure 25.7).

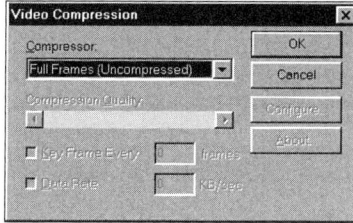

FIGURE 25.7
The Video Compression dialog box.

Higher video compression will create smaller exported files at the expense of movie quality. But compression can result in significant size reductions.

The process of exporting to QuickTime and Animated GIF are similar. Start the process by making the appropriate selection in the **Save As Type** drop-down menu.

INDEX

M

T